MW01690376

The N.U.D.E. Model

The New Art & Science of Referral Marketing

Scott Degraffenreid
Donna Blandford

Special discounts on bulk quantities are available to corporations, professional associations, and other organizations. Contact us for more details at:
www.donnablandford@aol.com

If there are any typos in this book they are there for a reason. Some people actually like finding them and reporting them. If you find any typographical errors report them back to donnablandford@aol.com. Thank you so much.

ISBN 0-9771738-0-1

Printed in the United States

Additional copies and e-books available at:
www.docmurdock.com

Special Thanks to Lisa Brooks for her creative book cover
(www.lisa@strawberrymoon.ws)

This book is dedicated to you, the reader.

It is all too easy for any of us, but especially business professionals to laps into familiar patterns, to stop learning, to believe that we know as much as we need to. Those of you taking the time to inquire and seek out new ideas, explore other possibilities, and consider how things are always changing are truly the reason we wrote this book. Thank you for your willingness to explore and be open to new ideas.

TABLE OF CONTENTS

Foreword vii
Preparing You To Read This Book vii
Acknowledgements xi
SOCIAL NETWORK ANALYSIS 4
Introduction 4
What is Social Network Analysis? 4
What do you do with Social Network Analysis? 7
The Definition of a Breakthrough 8
REFERRAL MARKETING 14
Information Overload 14
People are the New Media 16
The Power of Referrals 18
Why Referrals? 24
The Basic Model for Customer Referral Behavior 28
Novelty 29
Utility 32
Dependability 36
Economy 41
Tracking the Drivers 44
Backing into Your N.U.D.E. Number 58
Balance, Rolling the Diads 59
The Results are What Count 63
Breakthrough in the N.U.D.E. Model 63
REFERRAL BEHAVIORS 68
What are Referral Behaviors? 68

Get N.U.D.E. with Referral Behaviors 73
Creating Novelty 75
Creating Utility 84
Creating Dependability 87
Creating Economy 92
OPERATIONAL DISTINCTIONS 96
P.M.S. Makes It All Flow Together 96
P = Perception 97
M = The Message 101
The Looking Good Message (LGM) 103
Referrals and the Internet: 106
Show and Tell 107
S = Support 108
WORKSHEETS 114
WHERE DO WE GO FROM HERE? 120
INDEX 122

Foreword

Preparing You To Read This Book

My name is Donna Blandford and it has been my privilege to put the words on paper for this book. The biggest honor and blessing in my life is being married to Scott Degraffenreid. Yes, this book is a family affair.

Now you may ask why we have different last names. Well, I was a Blandford for 40 years before I met Scott and it is hard to change childhood behaviors plus I can barely spell Degraffenreid. Then hyphenating is out of the question. Donna Blandford-Degraffenreid, I don't think so. Scott likes to jokingly tell people I am on a ten-year probationary period. That always gets a chuckle.

That reminds me of one thing I wanted to share with you before you read too far. One of the biggest dilemmas I faced when we started this book was how much humor to add. I decided you would probably appreciate the excellent material and geeky perspective if you got a bit of our humor too. I hope you enjoy it.

Scott was raised in Oklahoma and his Okie colloquialisms are unique. If any of the humor offends you, I apologize in advance. He is usually simply trying to make a point in as playful a manner as he knows how.

The material we are delivering in this book has literally doubled business profits, launched companies into existence and enabled corporations to enter new markets with ease. The best news is that viral marketing is not expensive.

Referral marketing is not difficult. As we say over and over in the book it is so simple that it looks complicated. We designed the book to move you into creative action that will make your products and services stand out in the crowd and have your sales increased drastically through viral referral marketing. Most of the time this action will be talking to people in a certain way. So much of success happens in conversation.

The worst thing that could happen is that you read this book; you set it on a shelf and never map the material on to your products or services. We wrote this to support you in having an explosion of success. It won't do that unless you explore the material and apply the ideas to your projects. Scott asks many, many questions throughout this book. He expects you to answer the questions for yourself.

Scott presents this material often and much of this book came from his presentations. Many of the examples are participants in the workshops. Here are a couple of caveats we would like to get out of the way right at the beginning in the way of full disclosure. Since the Enron / World Com debacle, we think it is good to get all of our dirty laundry out of the way. So, here are a couple of things Scott says at the beginning of every presentation:

> *"I am severely hearing impaired and I depend somewhat on lip reading for full comprehension. So, if I don't respond to something you say, it doesn't mean I'm rude rather because I wasn't watching you. Actually, I am rude but I take all the slack I can get. It always bothered me that the hearing-handicapped don't get better parking privileges so I take the slack from that. I only park 3 or 4 times a day but I am rude a lot."*
>
> *"The other caveat is that I am not a professional speaker. I'm not a presentation guy of any kind really. I do 20 presentations a year and some of those are mostly "here's the report do you have any questions." So, don't expect a slick, glossy presentation."*

You may wonder why I include this in the book foreword. Well, Scott references some things in the book and having this information might make a bigger difference in your perspective. Perspective makes a huge impact in business. As you read this book you want to be continually exploring your perspective and consider the perceptions of your customers and the public in general.

We hope you find the book powerful and by reading this book, you make a big difference in your business or organization. Remember what Darwin said:

> ***"... in nature, nothing never works and nothing always works."***

Nothing works every time and some things are going to work even when it has never worked anywhere else before.

Well, that is all I can think to prepare you for this book. Let us know how this book makes a difference in your business. We also encourage you to ask us questions. Your questions lead us to new discoveries so feel free to email us at donnablandford@aol.com or go to our website at **www.NecessaryMeasures.com**.

Enjoy the book and start taking action on this material immediately.

Have a life you love!

Donna Blandford
August 30, 2004

Acknowledgements

Our next book will be on the subject of "acknowledgment" and how it shapes our lives. I'd need at least an additional book to more than superficially acknowledge the people I'll name here and two more books after that to even begin to acknowledge all those I haven't named but who have so immeasurably contributed to this effort.

I'll begin with B.J. and Lynn Dohrmann, the founders of IBI Global, simply and easily the most remarkable business networking organization in the world. Mr. Dohrmann's confidence in my ability to deliver this material coherently in front of large groups of people, despite my desperate admonitions that I don't really do presentations, is truly what made this book possible.

I love books. I read them voraciously and unapologetically. I'd much rather take time to read more of them than to write one. That's why I still haven't. The words you're reading now are literally the only ones that went through my hands to a keyboard. Much of the rest was transcribed from videos of my presentations at IBI's Free Enterprise Forums, where I have been honored to serve on their faculty, presenting the concepts of this book to entrepreneurs and CEO's at IBI's five events a year in Los Angeles (for more on this outstanding organization and to see old videos of some of my previous presentations, go to www.IBIGlobal.com).

I also owe the Dohrmann's my undying (in the most real possible sense of the word) gratitude for introducing me to Barry McKnew, inventor of The Life Vessel. This amazing alternative treatment device has freed me from the debilitating symptoms of Parkinson's disease, which was robbing me of not just my ability to function but my will to live. I no less owe my community of dear friends my eternal gratitude for urging and supporting me into trying something I couldn't scientifically understand or emotionally trust. Laughter may be the best medicine but sometimes suspension of disbelief is the water we should wash it down with. At the time of this writing The Life Vessel has no website. You can go to ours and look for the Life Vessel button for further info.

More than anyone else in the world I want to acknowledge the most wonderful person I've ever imagined, my dear and lovely wife and co-author, Donna Blandford. Her unflagging commitments to making this book happen, her tireless hours and thankless months of work are why you're reading this now. She took my meandering, arcane lectures and organized them into something comprehensible and structured. She also diligently and ruthlessly insisted I expand on those areas that were clear in my mind but nowhere else. That's just one of those things a good wife will do for you and I'm grateful beyond words for her.

I'd also like to acknowledge my many clients who have so graciously trusted these concepts to support and grow their businesses. Strangely, you might think, they are completely unnamed herein but that is my way of acknowledging them. The principles in this book work amazingly well but only when you can't see them working. To reveal my clients identities would, in several cases, significantly enhance the credibility of this book. Unfortunately it would also potentially compromise the value of work I've done for them if it were ever recognized as a "strategy". That makes my choice simple; the client always comes first. The anonymous examples herein are a combination of real and composites, some gleaned from volunteer coaching provided at IBI.

Strangely I'd like to acknowledge myself. My personal mantra is that "Everybody deserves a winnable game worth playing." and this book was written inside that commitment. To some degree, as a successful consultant, it could be persuasively argued that I'm better off keeping these secrets to myself for my clients. This isn't complicated stuff and nobody, as far as I know, has isolated some of these principles as clearly and completely as we have. So why write it? It could make a positive difference for someone, somehow. That's a good and noble reason but it's not mine. My reason is I'm writing this because I choose to. Living life as a choice isn't the only way to swim in a churning sea of explanations but I've found it's the easiest way to keep my head above water and my eyes on the far horizon. For that I acknowledge Landmark Education (www.landmarkeducation.com).

Lastly, I acknowledge you, our hapless reader. This book was written without benefit of professional editing. I freely acknowledge that, despite our best efforts, many errors of grammar, attribution, repetition and certainly omission, just to name a few, are still extant despite our and the little paperclip guy's from MS Word's attempts to ferret them out. I apologize and hope the benefits of applying this model to your business will in some small way counterbalance what may be a difficult or confusing read at times. Despite Donna's industrious and attentive labors this is basically raw "me". If, after reading this, you want me to speak to or consult with your organization, you should know what you see here is what you get. Don't say you weren't warned.

Respectfully,

Scott Degraffenreid
February 23, 2005

Embracing The N.U.D.E. Model

The New Art & Science of *Referral Marketing*

Scott Degraffenreid
Donna Blandford

SECTION ONE

SOCIAL NETWORK ANALYSIS

Introduction

Welcome to the world of Social Network Analysis and Viral Marketing. It is a very interesting world and it is my privilege to explore it with you in this book.

I want to take a few moments to introduce myself. Essentially, I'm a geek. I'm a Social Network Analyst, which you might think of as a very specialized form of Behavioral Statistics. You would be wrong but it is easier just to think of it that way. The differences should be apparent to you by the end of this book so lets not worry about it now. I like jobs that are so obscure that nobody knows if I'm doing a good job.

As a Social Network Analyst, for most of you, all you need to know is that I'm geekier than a sack of slide rules and I can complicate a glass of water. For the handful of you who want to know more, read the next section.

What is Social Network Analysis?

Social Network Analysis is one of the most exciting and important sciences you have probably **never** heard of. It has only emerged in the last 15 years as a result of huge advancements in computing capabilities and the ability to process really elaborate algorithms that can understand enormous patterns of behavior. It takes databases starting with one million data points and increasing to literally billions of data points to understand what people are going to do next in groups.

The nature of my work in Social Network Analysis has been very exciting the past several years because there have been some terrific advances in mathematics. To give you some idea how much mathematics has advanced in the last 10 to 15 years, the best parallel would be to take the entire history of flight, from the Wright brothers through the space shuttle to right now, including the Mars Probe and so on. Then compress that into just 15 years, that's what we've experienced recently in mathematics.

There have been a lot of major breakthroughs in the last 5 years. Not to bore you with this, because I will. The biggest breakthrough has been that there are now pilot versions of several new parallel intermaths that cannot be done by the human mind. In all of human history, math has been a function of what the human mind is capable of. Now computers can obviously do that math a lot faster. We now have new math that is capable of doing things that could never possibly be comprehended or done by the human mind.

This makes possible some really fantastic modeling of certain complex behaviors. Human behavior has always been of interest but the patterns that occur in large social networks have generally been too complex and difficult to quantify. Fortunately, thanks to those advances, we can now look at them with tools, algorithms, that allow us to extract information from extremely complex data sets.

My main work is not anything to do with marketing. I principally work with organizations showing them how to reduce employee turnover and increase productivity. My claim to fame in that area is that I've consistently been able to reduce voluntary turnover by at least 50% with commensurate increases in productivity usually of at least 20%. I've done that in over 100 organizations.

One of the things I was fortunate to work on when I was first transitioning into Behavioral Statistics was a project for a large pharmaceutical company. They wanted us to tell them why some physicians refer some drugs to their peers and not others. They had a terrific database of drugs that had been developed going back about 30 years. We had a large budget because it was a pharmaceutical company, which enabled great research. We were able to significantly impact their marketing of their drugs, but in the course of that project we looked at all types of referral behaviors.

When I chose to leave Forensic Accounting, my former profession, I had burned out on catching bad people and I wanted to work on keeping good people. So, I looked at a number of options for myself. I went to the library because I'm pretty good at doing my homework. Other than math, I've only got a couple of redeeming attributes such as I'm stubborn and I'm lazy but I will do my homework if it will save me time in the future.

So, I went to the library and I looked at the huge section of psychology and sociology books and they all had different ideas and different models. By pulling some of these books down at random, I noticed that they all disagree substantially on lots of important points. It is difficult to find any two psychologists who agree on three major points.

Then I happened to notice that off to one side and down a few rows there is this small section on animal psychology. There were maybe 20 books and they all agreed substantially on the major tenets of animal psychology. I got to thinking about this and there is an obvious reason – you can't ask the animals questions. All you can do is watch their behavior and from watching them, you come up with a pretty consistent model.

That's how I decided to get into Behavioral Statistics and eventually to specialize in Social Network Analysis which is a fairly recent innovation, a very specialized branch that uses some very specialized math to look at what happens and how resources and information move through a network. How they move more efficiently.

So, what we do in Behavior Analysis is observe people. There is a lot less guesswork. What we are dealing with is not explanations but rather predictions. Most of the purpose of Social Network Analysis is to develop predictive models so that we can see what is going to happen next. Predictions are what we are about. So, predicting what will get people to refer new business to you is what we are going to be talking about.

One of the first and most interesting things we noticed was that there was an almost perfect inverse correlation between the amount of advertising and advanced promotions of a drug and the amount of referral behavior. In other words, the more money they spent telling people about the new drug, the fewer doctors talked about it.

We explored everything we could think of that people were likely to refer. We were looking at everything that is frequently referred such as books, movies, restaurants, etc. By looking at the common characteristics when people refer something to someone we identified a very clear pattern. This pattern has made a huge difference in referrals for our clients.

What do you do with Social Network Analysis?

Now let's talk about what Social Network Analysis does. It is involved in many areas of today's world such as:

- Organizational Behavior

- Intra-organization Relations
- The Spread of Contagious Diseases
- Mental Health
- Social Support
- The Diffusion of Information
- Animal Social Organization
- Business / Market Development

One of the more interesting applications that I'm proud of, although I didn't participate in it, Social Network Analysis has been one of the most important tools in ferreting out the Al Quaeda network in the United States and around the world. By mapping the information flow and the dynamics of small isolated networks law enforcement agencies have been able to essentially shut down a lot of their communication. That gives you some sense of the versatility of such a young science.

I'm fascinated with all types of viral behavior. How information spreads through networks. We were able to identify the specific mechanics of referral behavior, in other words, how people perform the mental model that has them decide when they are going to refer anything to anyone else. We found that can be applied in almost any business.

The Definition of a Breakthrough

Bear with me as I digress a moment. I promise to get back to the useable, hands-on piece of this as soon as I can. Like many things, when you are dealing with complex data in very intricate systems, what you are looking for is simplicity. We are really trying to isolate the lowest common denominator, the simplest drivers.

What this book provides for is essentially what we hope will be "a breakthrough concept" for you.

> *__A Breakthrough Concept__*
> - *Is simple*
> - *Alters your perspective*
> - *Reveals new value-creation opportunities*
> - *Leads to discovery, creativity and excitement throughout the entire organization*
> - *If adopted, creates urgency and need for rapid change*
>
> *- Christopher W. L. Hart*
> *Author of* ***__Extraordinary Guarantees__***

A lot of what we are going to be discussing exists in the context of a breakthrough. It is so profoundly simple that you may overlook the value of it. Einstein said something really great that is often overlooked. It is probably one of his most important quotes. He said: "things should be made as simple as possible but no simpler." This is going to be really fundamental stuff. In fact, it will be so basic that a lot of you will think "this can not possibly make the difference I need it to in my business." It can and if you will give it a chance it will. Now let's look as each of these points that define a breakthrough:

- **A breakthrough concept is simple**

The thing that some times put people off is how simple it really is. Sometimes you are tempted to say: "Well, I knew that, that's obvious!" Edward DeBono said, "All the important ideas are obvious in retrospect." So, until you really get to use this, it's easy to dismiss it as "obvious" but you have to use it and see if it doesn't make a difference.

- **A breakthrough concept alters your perspective**

The other thing about this is that if you allow them in, they will alter your perspective. That's one of the major values I've found in reading and attending seminars. They are a way of acquiring new perspectives. You can almost see people shift in a lot of presentations when they realize where they have been operating from is exactly the source of all their issues, not any deficit of information or resources.

- **A breakthrough concept reveals new value-creation opportunities**

For example, most business owners think of their customers as bringing them business in the form of sales but inside a breakthrough concept of referral marketing it becomes apparent that customers are much more importantly their number one source of new customers. Understanding how to make your business a subject that people will be excited to tell their friends about becomes a primary and regular function of your daily accountability.

- **A breakthrough concept leads to discovery, creativity and excitement throughout the entire organization.**

It is obvious enough that referrals will have an impact on marketing strategy but a fully integrated breakthrough concept of referral marketing will just as clearly affect product development, service delivery, inventory management and sales training and development.

- **A breakthrough concept, if adopted, creates urgency and need for rapid change.**

Adapting a business to a referral based marketing approach cannot happen soon enough. The savings in advertising costs alone are incredible but the real benefit is in customer enthusiasm and loyalty.

Let me give you an example of this. Modern medical science is fortunate in that it has an identifiable birthday. Not every science can say that. But modern medical science can actually be traced back to a day in November in 1895 when a guy named Wilhem Roentgen accidentally left his keys on a photographic plate near an x-ray source. When that photographic plate was developed, the first medical application of x-rays for looking inside the human body was immediately exposed (pun intended).

Now that invention, in and of itself, doesn't constitute the breakthrough concept. What does is the notion that from that point forward modern medical scientists would look inside, beneath the surface, underneath what's obvious and apparent to what is underneath and inside. They have continued this rigorously even to modern times so that the evolution of x-rays through cat scans and all the advanced imaging technologies that we use today are a reflection of that one happy accident when a guy left his keys on a photographic plate.

Literally within 10 years of when x-rays became available, every medical textbook was being rewritten. Why? Because everything up to that point had been based on the superficial and the brief interventions of surgeries and autopsies. We were looking at the outside primarily and static bodies. So, it literally changed medicine. It was a breakthrough concept. There is probably no one around whose life hasn't been affected, if not saved, by the notion that we should look inside and underneath the surface rather than just outside. How that spread through modern medicine is a Social Network phenomenon.

It doesn't always work

Let me give you an example of how it doesn't always work, why things don't always take off. Do you happen to know the day the first helicopter flew? You may be familiar with the day the Wright brothers flew because that Centennial of flight was just a few years ago. It was 1903 for the Wright brothers. When was the first helicopter flown? It was 1907, just four years after the Wright brothers and literally concurrently with when the Wright brothers became visible and started flying publicly. Then we didn't hear anything from them for nearly 40 years. Helicopters were not widely used until the Korean War.

It was 40 years. What happened? We could postulate a lot of things but I think one problem was that helicopters did something that was already being done. They went up and down vertically. Hot air balloons were already doing that. They had been doing it for 200 years. So it was no big deal when helicopters came along. They thought, "oh, we already have something that does that, why do we need this?"

If you consider for a moment what if helicopters had advanced at the same rate as modern fixed wing aircraft and if they had been incorporated into the air transport system, we might not have huge sprawling airports in the middle of metropolitan areas. We could have shuttle systems using much more advanced vertical take-off and landing aircraft that would shuttle people efficiently and effectively from lots of points. It might have even changed the entire traffic pattern of major metropolitan areas. It might have changed a lot of important land use.

But it didn't happen. Why? Because of Social Networks, the conversations were not there to carry the concept forward. That's what Social Networks do, they move resources and information forward where it is needed and when it is needed. It didn't happen for the helicopter because of some latent and ungrounded assumptions. It goes up and it comes down, just like a balloon. Well, no it is not quite like that but the assumption buried it, at least for 30 or 40 years.

I have told you all this to make it clearer that what you are about to learn is not simply a more evolved version of what has always been known as "word of mouth" advertising. This is as different as the helicopter from a hot air balloon, quite literally. Where a hot air balloon is at the mercy of the wind and drifts more or less randomly, a Social Network Analysis derived referral model allows a precision of control and a degree of predictability never before possible.

SECTION TWO

REFERRAL MARKETING

Information Overload

Referral marketing has existed for years. Word of mouth is probably the original form of advertising or marketing as it were. But in recent history we have been overwhelmed. We have overlooked the value of word of mouth in favor of all the media.

Based on daily averages in an urban environment, conservative estimates say there are over 1,000 attempted intrusions or commercial requests for our attention per day. A lot of experts place that number even higher.

That figure reflects everything from television, radio, and newspaper advertising to blimps, billboards, pop-ups, and matchbook covers. From the time you open your eyes in the morning until you close them and fall asleep at night someone somewhere will be attempting desperately to obtain your interest in their product or service for just an instant. You are seeing lots and lots of requests for your attention to buy something, try something, experience something, etc. They may tease, shout, whisper, seduce, surprise, tempt, demand, bribe, or even outright try to trick us.

Because of the profligate inflation of advertising of all types, your attention however fleeting has become an incredibly valuable commercial commodity. Companies invest literally trillions of dollars to get you to look at them.

Unfortunately that investment has long since exceeded the point of diminishing returns.

What has happened is you have adapted your attention to filter out all that noise. Can you remember the last three ads you have seen today, what they wanted you to do or what they wanted you to buy? In a room of 150 people maybe 2-3 people can remember a couple of ads. That is amazing. If you consider all the millions of dollars of advertising and marketing that represents trying to get through to you. You have created very powerful filters that are keeping most of it out most of the time. You are not even conscious of that filter being on as you walk through life. Your mind is so powerful. It can attenuate almost anything.

It is like noise attenuation. You don't realize how much sound you are filtering at any moment, how much work your brain is doing at this very instant. If you are in a very noisy room, at first it occurs as a cacophony but if you are in there long enough, you start to focus on voices and the necessary information. Stop a moment and listen to the noises in the room, the music, the traffic, etc. And don't forget the air handlers, breathing, paper noises, clocks ticking, movement of clothing/jewelry, etc. There are number of noises but your mind is only looking for useful information. Your mind has also learned to attenuate that advertising and marketing as the same kind of useless information as the noises of the air handlers.

Your brain is enormously powerful. A lot of people are intimidated by math but you are doing an enormous amount of math right this very instant. Your brain is processing thousands of pieces of information, far more than just the words on this page. It is working to filter and process a lot of other noise and intrusions and let you focus on just the needed information. You are doing tremendous ratio calculations, analysis of covariance, lots of math that you would make you dizzy if you realized what was going on mathematically to allow you to function as well as you do.

You have got 30 billion brain cells in your cortex and they are connected by over a million billion connections, axons and dendrites and so on. In fact, it would take you 32 million years counting at one per second to count all those connections. That is going on inside your head right now. All those connections and all those cells are talking to each other at a staggering rate and you are attenuating all the information, a lot of the calculations, a lot of the thoughts and memories are being processed right now. Well, our brains have adapted to that cacophony of advertising, so we really let very little of it through.

So, it gets harder and harder for advertising to get through the filters. Even when it does rarely get through, we have come to believe that it is not accurate, so to speak. We have come to expect less than full integrity is present in a lot of advertising messages. It is Believe-ability Suspect for B.S. for short.

People are the New Media

So what is getting through? Personal endorsements, referrals, people willingly extending their credibility to a product or service they have experienced personally are the one remaining thing for which we will readily lower our shields. In a very real and important sense ***people are the new media***. We've become inured to most traditional media. What we are all generally open to are the recommendations, the advice and the suggestions of friends.

If you look at where you are getting information about your next buying decision, where you are likely to go to your next movie, your next restaurant or what books you are considering; for most of us it comes from your circle of friends, family and colleagues. This is where a lot of buying decisions are driven. If you have an endorsement by someone or even a negative endorsement (someone recommending against something), those endorsements are the most likely thing to influence your buying. Now you may not know anything about that person's expertise, qualifications or objectivity but you tend to lend it some credence because somebody took the time to tell you about it.

That does not mean you should ignore all the marketing strategies. It is absolutely important to have a marketing strategy and conventional marketing can be very valuable. We'll look at a couple of statistics that explain why you need both shortly. But it would be very dangerous for start-up businesses or small businesses to have only a conventional marketing campaign. If you can use viral endorsement behaviors, if you can get referrals, you absolutely should. And it is a shame if you can't.

There is a special relationship between referral marketing and conventional media) marketing. This may not make the traditional media works very happy but since I so seldom (as in never) buy TV, radio or newspaper advertising, I am willing to take that chance.

I am going to use the analogy of the horse and rider for this relationship:

- **The Horse** - Traditional media represents the horse. Big, powerful, hungry and very messy to keep inside (just kidding about that last part, I've met several media people who are almost completely housetrained).

- **The Rider** - Referral marketing is like a rider, it gives direction, training and care to the conventional marketing efforts.

Left unbridled, traditional marketing is often unable to arrive effectively at its objectives. It tends to wander and graze aimlessly, heading for the barn every chance it gets. Referral marketing by clearly identifying what the market finds attractive and interesting about a service or product achieves an efficiency of both direction and results otherwise only randomly available.

This by no means denigrates the horse. It can take you farther than the rider ever could alone. They can function as partners not unlike the Lone Ranger and his horse, Silver (I suppose this dates us but then again who else would?). Certainly Silver, on more than one occasion helped the Lone Ranger out of a jam. But at the beginning and end of every show, the Lone Ranger ALWAYS had to tell Silver where to go ("away" obviously). You would think that after hundreds of episodes Silver would start to get it and remember where he was going but not unlike conventional marketing, he has to be reminded every time that the market is in charge.

Absent this understanding and with a traditional media-only marketing approach, you can expect to see a lot of your own Silver going away and never coming back.

As to small businesses that may not need to go somewhere farther and faster, it is possible that the rider (referral marketing) can take you there alone. For the majority of our small clients, referral marketing is not just their primary; it is their exclusive marketing strategy. That doesn't mean they might not run an occasional newspaper ad or radio spot sometimes but it does mean they depend on referrals for 99.9% of their profitability and growth.

The Power of Referrals

I am sure all of you have heard of the impact of referrals but this is something we were only able to precisely quantify by looking at very large data sets. If we look at the force of the two relative channels that lead to buying (referrals versus advertising), the disparity is staggering.

The incidence of consideration is a term that addresses how often you defer to a referral or a piece of advertising when considering a purchase. It means you will at least think about comparing that product or service to other alternatives or choices. The statistics say that when somebody suggests something to you, you will consider that suggestion the next time you have an opportunity to buy or use that product 80% of the time. That is huge!

The incidence of consideration for a print ad, a full-page print ad, is less than 1%. Obviously the ROI (Return on Investment) is highly in favor of the referrals. In fact 1% is quite high. But if you consider the number of exposures, clearly it does get you some business. Quite a few people still read the newspaper. If you were to run a full-page ad in a newspaper, even a 1% incidence of consideration will get you some attention but that is only how many people will think about the product, still quite far from those who will become actual customers.

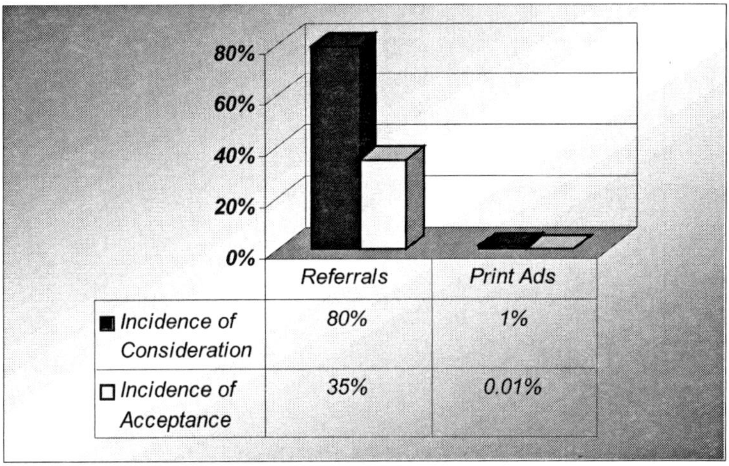

Referrals
>80% = Incidence of consideration
>35% = Incidence of acceptance

Print Ads
<1% = Incidence of consideration
<0.01% = Incidence of acceptance

The incidence of acceptance, some people call this the conversion rate, is when someone elects to purchase based on the referral or marketing. The incidence of acceptance from a referral is often over 35%. That means you are likely to buy one time out of three what people recommend to you. So over a third of the time the endorsement from a personal referral results in a sale.

Mind you, this number, as well as the incidence of consideration may vary widely according to numerous variables, not the least of which being the credibility or the relationship of the referring party. The variation is often remarkably positive. For restaurants referrals, for example, the incidence of acceptance can be well over 50%. With movies or television shows, the incidence of acceptance may reach an amazing 80% or more depending on what social networks receive the message. Of course we freely acknowledge that the incidence of consideration and acceptance for traditional media campaigns can exceed their average results by many times more. This is somewhat less impressive when you consider that a 500% improvement in incidence of acceptance still means you have only 0.10% versus 0.2% expected.

If a newspaper has a circulation of one million then an advertisement would have an incidence of consideration of around 10,000 people considering the product or service resulting in sales of 200. Consider how you can leverage old media (traditional) with the new media (people). If you had viral referral behaviors and those 200 people brought you 10 new customers then that advertisement could be compared to a circulation of ten million.

Now, compare and contrast that with all other marketing combined, I don't mean individually, I mean combined. When you take everything put together your total incidence of consideration for all media combined is 1.5%.

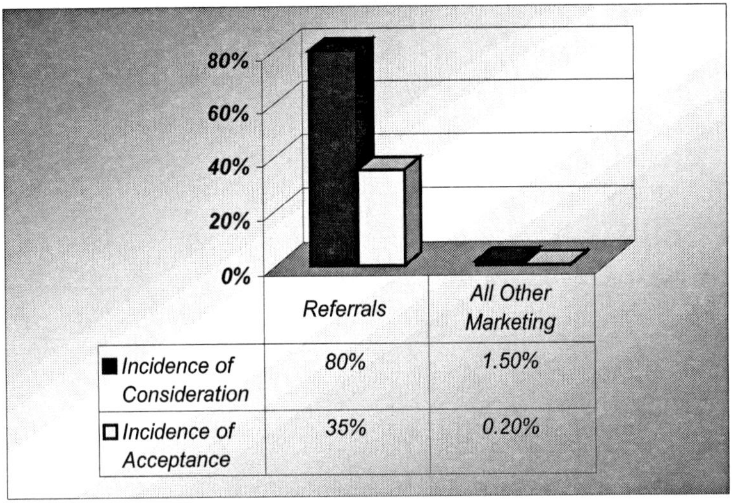

<u>Referrals</u>
>80% = Incidence of consideration
>35% = Incidence of acceptance

<u>All Other Marketing</u>
<1.5% = Incidence of consideration
<0.2% = Incidence of acceptance

Once again, you cannot completely disavow conventional marketing and advertising because it can reach millions of people. It is a numbers game. 0.20% does not sound like much unless you are talking about millions of exposures. So if you are Sony or Nike or Sprint, 0.20% is not such a bad uptake. But for most of us who have smaller markets, it is not an especially good value because the cost for all those exposures is exorbitant in most cases.

With 1,000 exposures, there would be 15 people who would consider your product or service. That's even briefly considering it. For a newspaper with a readership of 200,000 that equals 3,000. The incidence of conversion or acceptance is 0.02%. Now, 0.02% of 1,000 is 0.2. So that means approximately every 5 days you buy something based on marketing or advertising. That is about 73 times a year.

Does that surprise you? Do you think you actually buy something 73 times a year based on marketing and advertising? These statistics are based on product tracking surveys. We look at how much advertising is going on and then how much product sales. It's again, empirical evidence. Mathematical evidence is what leads us to that estimate.

The incidence of acceptance from a print ad is significantly lower, usually less than 0.01% with the exception of, perhaps, grocery ads. But that is still very low in comparison to the referral statistics.

It is obviously becoming more and more difficult to break into people's attention. The attempted incursions on our attention have been quoted as high as 5,000 a day. So we are exposed to up to 5,000 advertising messages and encroachments on our thinking and it is very difficult to sort through that. About the only way to break through it is through a personal endorsement. That's the fastest, surest way to penetrate the barriers that we are naturally building.

Often, I say that I am not particularly good at marketing myself, at least not by conventional standards. I am not good but I am effective. I live on referrals. I don't have any other marketing strategy but I've done okay with that. I'm not any form of marketer, in fact I used to say, only half jokingly if I have any "marketeer" blood in me, get a knife and let it out. Although I have the greatest respect for marketing professionals, I didn't want to be branded a marketer.

I have done a lot of survey research over the years. The thing I learned in doing survey research is that even the best surveys are very unreliable. That's why I'm basically a Behavioral Statistician; I don't do a lot of survey statistics because of the problem we refer to as response error.

Let me give a somewhat exaggerated example. If you ask a group of people: "How often do they brush their teeth?" You are going to get an answer such as 2-1/2 to 3 times a day. But if you actually measure the amount of toothpaste used, you would know immediately that someone is lying. We don't call it lying we call it response error.

Sometimes we can correct for response error. We know how much toothpaste is being used and we know approximately how much toothpaste people use for brushing so we can quantify the lie and build in a correction for it.

For a lot of things, we don't have good measures for response errors, which makes the surveys very difficult and unreliable, particularly for things like referral behavior. If we ask people something, we get one set of answers but what we've done here is actually watch their behavior.

Why Referrals?

The interesting thing that we recognized early on when looking at the data from the pharmaceutical study where we were researching physicians' referral patterns was that the new drugs that had the greatest advertising and marketing exposure, that had been in all the major journals and had debuted at all the big conferences had the least referrals. The drugs that had trickled in, that had very little exposure had the highest incidence of referrals. Isn't that interesting.

It was very valuable for the pharmaceutical company to know this because they realized very early on that they had been spending millions and millions of dollars for smaller and smaller results in most cases. We looked at more than 60 drugs over a period of about 25 years and in every single case the small drugs with limited exposure had greater word-of-mouth and terrific burn through in viral referrals. The ones with splashy marketing campaigns costing millions of dollars had very slow penetration in the market because there were almost no peer endorsements.

Here's a simple question for you. I also refer to this question as the million-dollar question. **Why do people refer things to people?**

Why Do People Refer? So someone will think they look good!

One of the first things we discovered when we were doing the research for the pharmaceutical company was that referrals are basically a very simple phenomenon as are most of the things in my field. We refer anything to anyone in order to enhance our standing with the person being referred.

So, very basically and very simply, **we do it to look good**. We can determine that by looking at the behaviors and testing in several different ways but we are pretty clear that this is the core driver. It is very basic but it is critically important and we will come back to it time and time again as we explore referral marketing. If it does not give someone an opportunity to look good then they are not going to talk about it.

For example: if you hear about an alternative medicine but you are skeptical about it. Will you refer it? Most people will not refer until they know it works and then they will look good. If it does not work, they do not look good and that is embarrassing.

Of course, some people resist that, they say: *"oh no, I do it to help my friends and the people who really deserve it. I have no consideration for myself, I'm just doing it completely altruistically."* But for most businesses, you can't just count on those few people who are doing it altruistically. You have to depend on those who are doing it to look good also. You really need that to work for you.

People may be uncomfortable about all this talk about looking good but to get a little biblical with you for a moment: *"Consider the lilies of the field, they sow not, neither do they reap..."* but they do something very important and quite germane to our conversation here. Flowers are very much a ''looking good' thing but they have been succeeding prolifically for over a billion years. Flowers exist specifically to attract birds and insects that will carry their genetic information for cross pollination and propagation. They enable species to expand, mutate and flourish but they have to stand out and look good to do that.

In much the same way our innate human desire to look good enables businesses to flourish and succeed. It is nothing to be embarrassed about. Not only is it a perfectly natural act, it is a powerful catalyst for a thriving free market economy. Of course since a flourishing free-enterprise system is both a powerful inducement for and a support for democracy it is not that much of an exaggeration to say our vanity is helping to defend the Constitution.

Author's note: It would make me really happy if you hummed an appropriate John Phillips Sousa tune while re- reading this preceding passage.

Then the next question becomes more complicated, **how do we decide what makes us look good?** That's an interesting question that we will spend most of the rest of this book exploring.

How do people decide they will look good? How do they decide they will look smart by referring you to something? What are the characteristics that we use to make that mental assessment? If I were guessing, I'd never get thc answers to these questions. This is why it's so good to have math. It turns out the answer is just another calculation.

Remember you have got those 30 billion brain cells working like mad all the time, mostly trying to think how you are going to look good. How do they decide? They are doing a lot of complex calculations. You just don't have any way of checking it because you don't know what the variables are. All we need to know is what are the variables in making that calculation called "what will make us look good" and we can drive peoples' perceptions. Now again, as with everything we are talking about here, this is nothing but a perception. There is no reality, it is what people think but what we think is what is real.

How many things can come into play, how many things can be a factor? What are the criteria that help us decide whether we look good? How do you know it will make you look good?

Let's back up to when I was talking about being bad at marketing. In science, there is a tendency to naming something after the discoverer and they don't always have good names. You've probably heard of the Bernoulli Principle but you don't automatically remember that it's what keeps an airplane in the air or the Leidenfrost Effect that enables you to walk across hot coals without getting burned or Avogadro's Number, etc. You can't really remember what they are for, so I decided that I'm not going to name this the Degraffenreid Model. As catchy a name as that is, I decided not to use that. Fortunately, it had a very interesting acronym, which amused me at the time and still does.

It is the N.U.D.E. model. Now I ask you, how often do you get to explore a N.U.D.E. model. Although, be careful because your spouse might get upset if you casually drop the N.U.D.E. model into your dinner conversation. It might get you in trouble.

The Basic Model for Customer Referral Behavior

Yes, how often do you get to name something the N.U.D.E. Model and have the acronym work?

We went through the original database of candidates with over 300 drivers and did the analysis of covariance and other geeky stuff, isolating around 60 properties for testing. What we found ultimately were there are actually 4 properties that had to be present in a certain combination that would predict the likelihood of referral behavior. It was very clear and very quantifiable. Now we will talk about those properties and how you can build them into your business models, into you products and services.

I'm going to go over each one. As we do, think of the last time that you referred anything to anyone or when anyone referred something to you and look and notice how these properties were or were not present.

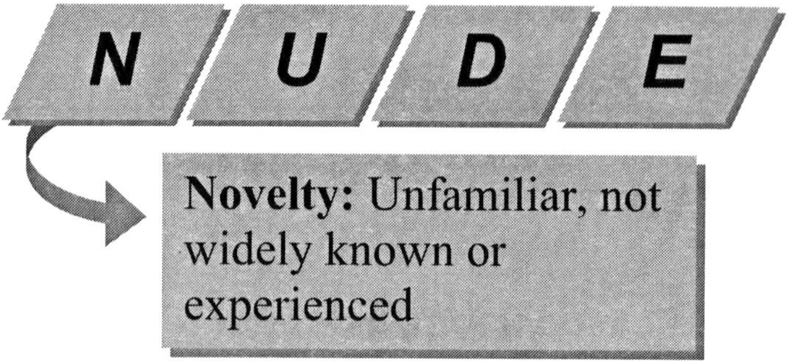

Novelty

The first and probably most challenging driver is Novelty. If everyone has already heard of it then it is not (generally) novel, there is no reason to refer it to someone. This is obvious right? If someone came up to you and said: "hey have you heard of McDonalds?" You might laugh in their face because, of course, you have heard of it. Everyone is going to have heard of it and recognize it.

So, the thing that we are most anxious to tell people about is something that we know they are not likely to have heard about or not known about before. Now you may be fortunate enough to have products or services that people have not heard of before but even if you have a very familiar product, you can attach Novelty to it. We are going to talk about how to do that in an upcoming chapter. It is really critical that you have Novelty, without at least a moderate degree of Novelty almost nothing qualifies for a referral.

> You have got to preserve your Novelty

It is unfortunate that people are usually looking at how most things are similar to everything else. Therefore, given a chance, people will look at your product or service and say, "oh, this is sort of like that." You have got to stop them before they do that. You have got to preserve your Novelty because that is essential to word-of-mouth referrals and viral marketing. Keeping them from lumping you with something they have seen before is half the job in most cases.

There is almost no amount of time that you can spend on Novelty that won't be well spent. Remember you can actually, it turns out, have Novelty be present in some degree with almost any product, all the time, even old established products.

When a new movie comes out, it is novel; there is a lot of referral activity around it. When a restaurant is new, there is a lot of referral activity. This is deceptively simple because we assume that it is only things that are new that will benefit from that type of referral activity. On closer examination Novelty is more often just a tempered phenomenon.

There are two basic types of Novelty:

1. **Fresh Novelty**
   The obvious Novelty is Fresh Novelty. That is just because it is recent. It hasn't existed up until that point. No one has heard of it because it is just simply new.

   > Fresh Novelty must be renewed or recreated regularly.

   - A new movie
   - A new book
   - A new restaurant

   That's easy but it wears off quickly. It is inherently transient. You cannot depend on Fresh Novelty after something has been out for a while.

2. **Contextual Novelty**
   There is an easier kind of Novelty to sustain. Contextual Novelty is significantly different or unusual relative to competing products or services such as:

Contextual Novelty can be preserved and/or defended indefinitely.

- Southwest Airlines
- Starbucks
- Amazon.com

There are a lot of products and services that can claim and sustain Contextual Novelty because they stayed different from their competition in some visible and compelling way. Amazon.com obviously started out with Fresh Novelty but sustained Contextual Novelty by dominating their field.

Essentially, you want something that is distinctive about your business or product that gives people a chance to tell their friends and family about you that makes them look good because they would not have heard of it before. And it stays that way over a long period of time and you can defend it. Clearly no one has been able to encroach significantly on Southwest Airlines, Starbucks or Amazon.com because they have distinctive features that they have manage to preserve and defend over time. We will talk a lot more about how you can create and preserve Contextual Novelty in future chapters.

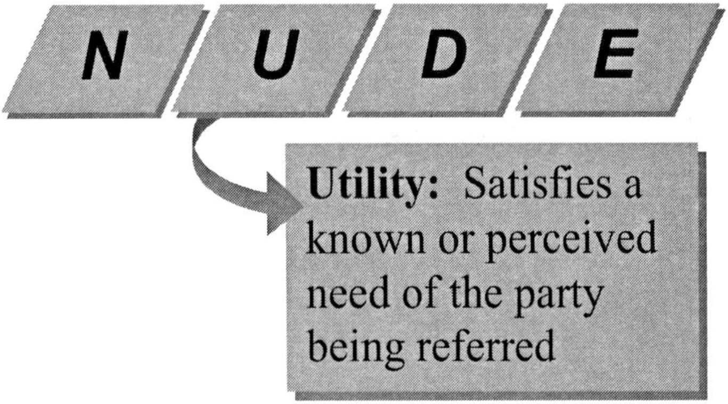

Utility

The next aspect that people are constantly calculating in their mental assessment is Utility. In other words, will the majority of the people you mention it to have a use or a need for it. That's also not terribly difficult. You wouldn't refer a pool service to someone who lives in a trailer park. It has low Utility there. You need to have some idea that they need it.

Unlikely Referrals due to low Utility:

- A feed store to an apartment dweller
- A video store to a blind man
- Donald Trump to a thrift shop

You would never think to mention these things to these people. You have to consider whether people will see the Utility in it.

Likely Referrals due to high Utility:

- A carpenter to a lumber yard
- A lawyer to someone getting a divorce
- A restaurant to someone who is hungry

Now there is a problem between Novelty and Utility. Often if something is very novel we do not see it as very useful. But that is a preview of an upcoming chapter.

Utility may seem simple and obvious until you really start to look at it. For instance, some things have such general Utility that they really don't have any natural target. In other words, there is no one specific person that you may want to tell about something. As a classic example, restaurants have such general Utility because everyone eats and almost everyone eats out from time to time.

Ideally when you are exposed to a product or service you will think immediately of whom you will want to tell about it. But because of the broad general utility of restaurants, hotels, gas stations, dry cleaners, etc; no one person or group comes immediately to mind (of course these may also lack significant Novelty as well). You don't really know who to mention one to unless it is in the context of a particular neighborhood where they live or work or it is a particular type of restaurant that you know someone enjoys.

To attain a perception of more specific Utility and thereby a more focused target for referrals, a restaurant may want to emphasize one or two specific Utilities. For example:

- A meeting room available for business groups so that a customer would think of acquaintances they know who have regular meetings
- A diabetic menu because many people know friends or family who are diabetic
- Add vegetarian items, although I personally am a huge fan of meat, I like many vegetarian dishes, especially when they are made with fresh vegetarians because they

are so tender. Incidentally does it bother anyone else that the "free" range chicken is more expensive?

- As an even better example, although many restaurants now offer low carb menus, a table service restaurant that usually brings bread or crackers before the meal could simultaneously attain Novelty and Utility by offering an option of a small veggie plate rather than a bread basket.

Think of how many people you know who are on low carb diets that you would mention the last option to? That is Specific Utility.

Now keep in mind, as with each of the four attributes, Utility is just a perception. It isn't whether your product or service is useful or needed it is whether your customer is guided to think of who they know that they think will have a use or a need. Everyone assumes their product or service has Utility but to do so without accepting accountability for specifically who will need it, they cheat themselves out of many potential referrals.

Ideally you should think of at least three groups or specific social networks that you would like to be referred to and consider what would constitute specific Utility for those groups. I encourage many of my consulting clients to think of at least one new target constituency per month and how they could position themselves to demonstrate Utility clearly and concisely for that network. Then write when they are going to do that directly into their calendar (schedule) so there is action to move them forward.

There are dozens of potential specific Utility networks for nearly every business. Many businesses may have hundreds or even thousands of Specific Utility Networks. It's obvious they have to have a use or a need for it for the Utility to be high. They are natural referrals that fit. You have to perceive they have a need for it.

Wherever possible, it is best to target networks that are both broad and deep. A broad network, very simply, is one with a large number of members. The more critical aspect however, is depth; this represents the frequency of communication within this network or their structures for sharing information. As an example, short people are a relatively large group in number (ha ha) but they are barely considered a network because they have no system or formal structure for communication.

A better example of a network that is narrower but relatively quite deep would be golfers. Not only do fellow golfers frequently discuss their sport, they have magazines, television shows, newspaper columns and specific locations to indulge their interest. Even though they are less easily identified than short people, they are usually known to be golfers even by friends and family who are non-golfers.

So to return to our example of restaurants, a happy hour putting contest would be something you would be eager to mention to a golfing friend. Or as another example, a putting for pie contest where a patron who has had four or more people for dinner would have a chance to sink a 30' putt for a slice of pie.

Some of you may see these types of suggestions as Novelty, as you will see later when we discuss the concepts of diads, Novelty and Utility are companions of a sort, always in a dance with each other. In many cases when we are talking about the referral model, Novelty and Utility are a sort of mirror image that effectively magnify each other. But if not managed carefully can just as easily cancel one another out.

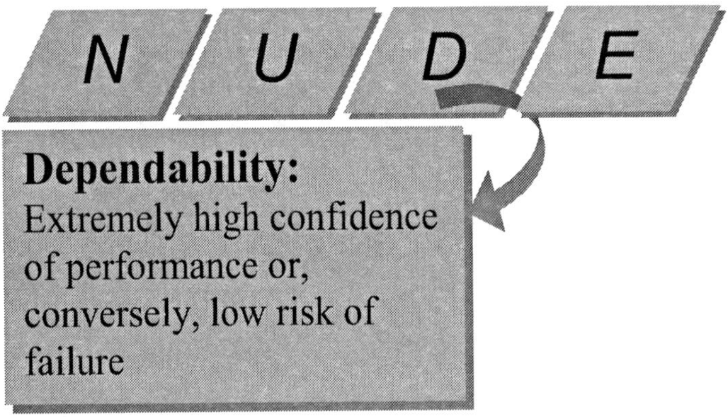

Dependability

The third characteristic is Dependability. This kills a lot of referrals. People have no idea how much damage this does to their potential for referral marketing. If something is seen as unreliable or as inconsistent you will not refer it. Why not? It would not make you look good. If you know of a restaurant and it had great service one day and great food the next but never at the same time you will not send people there.

By the way, what kills restaurants in the long haul is the fact that in the beginning the Novelty captures peoples' attention but as time goes on and the Novelty wears off the focus goes to those detail things that were probably out of alignment the first time and you did not notice it because it was the first time you were there. Therefore, it is very difficult for restaurants to obtain and preserve a reputation for Dependability when they start off with this big splashy Novelty. There are ways of correcting that but we will save that for a later date.

One important thing about Dependability is that a high confidence of performance refers to **expected** performance. A lot of people confuse Dependability with being infallible.

It is not that it is 100% failure free but rather that it performs exactly as expected. Said another way: if something performs exactly as expected does not mean it is 100% reliable.

What is the most successful retail chain in the world? The answer is Wal-Mart. Now is their service superlative? No, as a matter of fact, now I have to check myself out, after I can't find the thing I came for, I have to figure out how to pay for it. How much service is that? And yet they are the biggest retail corporation in the world. Why? Because no one is treated any differently there and you know exactly what you are getting into

Is it absolutely dependable? No, but it is dependably mediocre. This is important. You see a lot of people get screwed on these "Knock your socks off" service excellence concepts. If you get committed to some "knock your socks off" service idea, you are creating expectations that are very often difficult to maintain and fulfill.

Wal-Mart has hit a nice, medium, even keel, mediocrity and nobody else gets better than that mediocrity and nobody gets worse than it so everyone is okay with it. You are not surprised to stand in line for 5 minutes because you stood in line for 5 minutes the last time and you will probably stand in line for 5 minutes the next time. That kind of Dependability though is all you need (Not that Wal-Mart is a high candidate for referrals). I am not advocating mediocrity here. I am just telling you that people have to know what they can expect and get it every time. They don't have to get perfection.

Another classic example is McDonalds. How is their service? It is not quality service and the person waiting on you may not look you in the eye or speak your language. But you know what you are going to get every time. Inconsistency, not incompetence, is the opposite of Dependability.

Even if something is weak in regards to service but strong in selection and/or pricing, the referrer can prepare the referral party for that shortcoming such as: *"you have to try this it is a great price and the selection is wonderful but plan to have to wait for your order."*

You are once again dealing with perception when you deal with Dependability. For example lets say you have a product in the alternative health care products field. Now let me say this emphatically so you hear me that there is nothing wrong with your Dependability. I will say it again I am not saying there is anything wrong with your Dependability as far as I know. However, you are in a poisoned well because there are a lot of ineffective alternative health care products out there, a lot of unreliable products out there. It is not that these don't work but they make spurious, undocumented and unsupported claims. As soon as you get into the same bucket, alternative health care, you are stuck with the rest of them. Your Dependability is as suspect as anyone else's.

Therefore, you have got to find a way of detaching yourself, like climbing out of that poisoned well so that you are not in the same bucket with everyone else that is offering a money-back guarantee if it doesn't kill you. People think that makes it okay because they have a money-back guarantee. Well, why would you need one if it works? Everyone who has a product that is suspect thinks that a money-back guarantee is a way out of that but it is not because everyone who's product is suspect has a money-back guarantee. You are basically just climbing in the same bucket with everyone else and creating the same expectations.

Dependability is a little like Utility, in that most businesses have a difficult time objectively assessing how their customers *perceive* their Dependability. On a day-to-day or average experience basis most businesses can feel reasonably good about their Dependability. Unfortunately most businesses' customers do not experience their service or product on a day-to-day basis. And clearly no *one* experiences average service.

Here is the tricky part. Customers are never comparing their current experience of your product or service with their previous experience of your product or service. What they are comparing, and this is crucial, is their memory of their previous experience. That is how people access Dependability and even though it is a very subjective comparison that can be influenced by numerous variables, if it is understood, it can be managed.

Going back to the classic example of restaurants, any time spent waiting for a table or service almost always seems greater in the current moment than in our memory of previous experiences. Now why is that? Well, basically waiting is uneventful; there is nothing to distinguish it or give it a placeholder in our memory. We nearly always think it takes longer to be seated or get our order when we are waiting than we remember it taking the last time we were there.

This clearly puts almost any business that delivers service at a disadvantage in terms of customers' perceptions. So, how can they manage this? There are several ways. One is to let people know each time, approximately how long the delay or interval will be and then acknowledge when that target is or is not met. For instance: when you sign in at the doctor's office, if they tell you the wait will be 15 minutes or less and then when they call your name if they said *"I apologize for the delay, I hope we haven't kept you waiting any longer than we promised."* How would you feel? For most people that experience is far preferable to waiting for an unknown period and not having it addressed at all.

Another way of managing the perception of delays is to offer a tangible token of apology such as when you go to the drive-thru window of a restaurant and you are asked to pull forward and wait, many offer a coupon for a free drink on your next visit.

One big problem with Dependability actually has to do with its relationship to Novelty. When you first experience a product or service, your attention will be on the unfamiliar aspects or distinctive differences. Essentially you are distracted from the ordinary by whatever is novel. Now the problem with that in regards to Dependability is that in subsequent experiences your attention is no longer focused on the unfamiliar and you may become aware of details that have not changed from the previous experience but which were simply unnoticed. That isn't the way we perceive it though. We don't think to ourselves "gosh I didn't notice it that way before," we think "it wasn't that way before" therefore, this is undependable.

This issue of "perceived Dependability" is what kills restaurant referrals en masse, leading to the common referral pattern known as "Bottle Rocket" effect. This is a phenomenon where initially there is a very, very high occurrence of referrals but as a result of the returning patrons' *perception* that something is inconsistent; referrals drop off exponentially, hence the reference to the rapid rise and precipitous fall of a bottle rocket.

There are several ways of beating the Bottle Rocket Effect. One is to keep people distracted by continually introducing new elements, changing artwork regularly, adding a mirror, moving furniture, adjusting the menu, etc. Another is to simply take things away, for example removing a large plant, taking out a wall, taking away a mirror, etc.

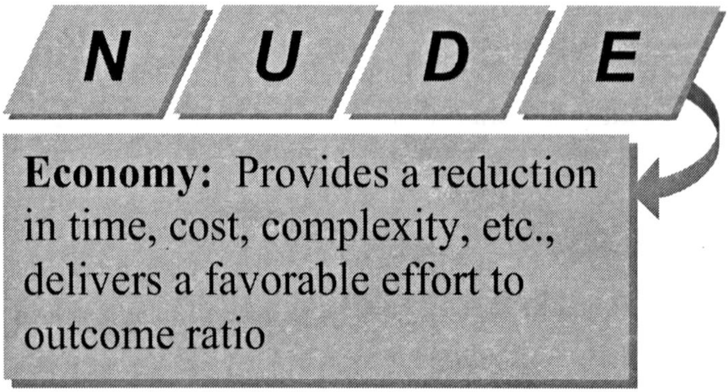

Economy

The fourth characteristic that we are continuously, subconsciously calculating in our brain is Economy. Economy does not mean cheaper necessarily. It is just that it has a better value and you get more of what you wanted out of it. Don't get confused with inexpensive or lower priced when we talk about Economy.

Very often what you get out of Economy is image. It enhances something about yourself, some story about yourself, some position in the social network that you are seeking that the product helps you attain quicker, better, or safer than the alternatives.

You often get more of the approval you are looking for, keeping in mind that most purchases of almost any kind are a social phenomenon. We are not really buying products and services we are shopping for approval. You buy things partly because they fit the story you have about yourself but also because they get people to think of you in the way that you want to be thought of. That's what drives most of your shopping behavior even in professional considerations.

Strangely, a Hummer is going to be economical for some people. Now that may not make much sense on the surface. There are few vehicles as ludicrously expensive to own and operate as a Hummer. However, there are also very few vehicles that get the kind of attention a Hummer gives. So, as a form of transportation, the Hummer may not rate very highly. But as an ego support system and overall attention-getter, it is economical because, simply put, it gets them what they want at a price they are willing to pay.

Many people happily spend more for brand name products they are familiar with rather than generic or store brands. The Economy here is actually a function of what they perceive as Dependability. They are willing to pay more in order to attain a predictable result. Products and services are almost never referred primarily because of their Economy unless they are what we refer to as transparent undifferentiated commodities.

Transparent means that it is generally not noticed unless it fails or seriously under performs. An example would be your cellular phone service or Internet service provider. Undifferentiated refers to the fact that there are no immediately discernible differences in quality or style. Commodity simply means that it is something that is needed by a fairly large group of people on a regular basis.

Gasoline therefore is to most people a transparent undifferentiated commodity. In some cases, products such as this, especially when prices may have recently escalated, may be referred if they are significantly lower in price. In actual practice, because such products are generally sold with relatively narrow profit margins, wide disparities in price are not likely to last for long.

As an example, if I find a gas station where the price is 10-15 cents/gallon lower than other stations for the same grade that may be sufficient for me to refer it to someone. However, because such price disparities generally don't last, I am only likely to refer it for a short period of time or as long as I can be reasonably certain that price will remain.

Economy has a better value relative to what we have been using even if that was nothing. It has a better value than the alternatives. It is often decided by convenience or lower effort, rather than price, it can be as simple as getting the same thing in less time. Fundamentally it is about getting more of something we want for less of something we are willing to exchange.

Convenience is often the deciding factor in Economy. For instance if there is a closer dry cleaning store or a closer grocery store or department store, there is an Economy related to the location because it takes less time and effort.

> Once again, as always, it is a looking good thing.

To some people there is what we refer to as the economics of loyalty. They may use the same provider for years and frequently refer to how long they have had the same hair stylist, etc. In this case they may refer their long-term supplier simply to have an opportunity to mention how long they have used them. What they get from this is an image of loyalty.

There is one more Economy and we will call it the Economy of Relationship. We could also call this "A friend on the inside" phenomenon. When you have a relationship with a provider of any kind in which you know more than just their name and they know more about you than just your name. There is a greater tendency to believe that you would be missed if you were to choose another provider. In this type of Economy it is the value you provide as a customer to the provider rather than the value the provider is offering you. Being valued and known is worth something to many people. It can also be an experience that your customers will want to share (refer) with others.

Tracking the Drivers

So, these are the 4 attributes. And people form calculations that estimate these properties before they refer almost anything. How I know this is because I have looked at literally hundreds of products and services and quantified the presence or absence of those characteristics and looked at the level of referral behavior. Now, it's a lot more complicated than that but that is basically how I know this.

They are all quantifiable. Those properties are always present in a certain measure. This is what is really important. We need to know how we can track this. In my world, data always has decimals. There are always numbers on it. So, the way that we measure these things is again deceptively simple. It takes no more math than it takes to balance your checkbook.

You can assess your business very quickly and see how close you are to having a viral referral strategy.

- 100% **Novelty** is when nobody you mention it to has ever heard of it before. That is very difficult to reach. For instance with Fresh Novelty, your erosion is probably 2-3% per day minimum so you only have Fresh Novelty for about 30 days on any given product or service. Because every day a few more people hear about it. If half the people you told had never heard of the product it would be a score of 50%.

- 100% **Utility** means everyone you mention it to has a use for it. Not that everyone has a need or use for it but everyone that you would think to mention it to knows someone who has a need or use for it. That is 100%. It is also relatively rare but it is available to a lot of products. For example, a new golf store in town has a Fresh Novelty but it only has Utility for golfers.

- 100% **Dependability** means it works as promised or expected every time. If it works as expected half the time that would be 50%. It is that simple. Remember peoples' perceptions color this one very quickly making 100% very difficult to attain in Dependability.

Even if we have a failure rate of say 1% but it failed the last time you used the product, the perception is that it is very undependable and not reliable. So, Dependability erodes exponentially. One failure can be perceived as a very high failure rate if it occurred the last time the product or service was used. Dependability erodes exponentially but is only recovered incrementally. If the customer takes the time to use the product or service again, you can recover the Dependability by not failing or disappointing them again but it is seldom that easy.

For some businesses losing the customer's confidence, their perception of Dependability is like losing your virginity. It is not coming back.

In those unfortunate instances where it is clear that perceptions of Dependability have been badly compromised, it may be necessary to take extreme measures to recover it.

Extraordinary Guarantees - One tool for doing so has been described brilliantly by Christopher W.L. Hart in his book "Extraordinary Guarantees." I encourage you to find and read closely this currently out of print but generally available book if your business is confronted with Dependability issues. This is by no means a substitute for reading the book but as a very compressed summation of this excellent concept, what it amounts to is putting more at stake in a guarantee than you can be comfortable with. As I have said previously "a money-back guarantee is not especially valuable or impressive." All you have done by giving me a money-back guarantee is restore me to my original condition prior to using your product or service minus whatever time, effort or inconvenience plus the frustration of using something unsatisfactorily.

Here is the problem with guarantees. Everyone has a money-back guarantee or some sort of satisfaction guarantee. You have got to go over the top for a guarantee to have any possible impact on the perception of Dependability.

You have to put some skin in the game. If you give back their money, you are not out anything. They got their money back and you got the product back or maybe not. In order to get an extraordinary guarantee to work you have got to really be out there such as 150-200% guarantee. Now that is scary but it says something about your commitment to satisfaction. Now, there are more and more companies doing that so you have to get with that before long because it gets eroded. Eventually as people see that really does work they will start to see that they actually gain from the guarantee and that your product or service really does work.

Your product has to be good to give an extraordinary guarantee. It just has to be like every other product in town to offer an ordinary money-back guarantee. People expect their money back if it doesn't work. It does not accomplish anything to give them what they had before, which is their money back. You have got to not only make them whole but better than they were. That goes for almost everyone who has a guarantee that is contingent on the dependability of the product. Now, I don't necessarily say that guarantees are the only way to establish the dependability of a product.

Live endorsements are the surest way to influence the perception of Dependability. If you are living viral and you have referrals then that establishes the Dependability of the product. If you have to go and tell people about it, the dependability is automatically suspect. You can talk all day about the quality of your product but when someone else praises your product, it helps define your product's Dependability.

In a sense, this is one of those "nothing-succeeds-like-success" phenomena. The more referrals you have, the more people will perceive you as dependable. The more dependable you look, the more referrals you will have.

The best thing you can do for written referrals (testimonials) is to put a face with them. People trust faces, so get peoples' pictures up on your website and in your brochures because names are nothing and faces are everything. Our brains are hard wired to trust and recognize faces. Information that comes from faces is about 200% more credible than other stuff.

First hand, warm-blooded face-to-face recognition and endorsement is worth more than all the rest put together.

A number of companies have been attempting to use the Internet for what they refer to as Social Network Marketing. Typically they will have paid endorsers go to chat rooms and blogs and recommend or tout some product or entertainment property. In the short term, this may influence a few people but as this practice becomes more widespread, most people will become aware of it and grow just as skeptical and oblivious to it as any other paid advertisement. I have actually been in chat rooms when a participant was called out for this type of behavior and asked to leave. I expect advertisers will discover, that even worse than being ineffective, these "bought-and-paid-for" referrals may even engender a negative backlash among parties who recognize the manipulation.

Dependability for all types of businesses is the great bug-a-boo, the one that kills more businesses than any other in terms of referrals because if they think it might fail, if there is any concern that it might not perform as expected will not refer it. Why not? Because it won't make them look good!

- 100% **Economy** means that it is always recognized as a better value. This one is not as tough as it sounds but it does require some positioning.

The perception of Economy is a funny thing. People like a story with their Economy. They like to know the reason something is a better value. Outlet malls are a remarkably successful example of this phenomenon. People like to believe that eliminating the middleman, buying directly from the manufacturer means they are buying goods that would cost much more in a retail store. Never mind the fact that many of the things they buy in factory outlet stores are no longer sold at retail because they are closeouts or seconds.

It is the perception that counts. In this case the perception is grounded in the back-story. In this instance, you cannot be just "**cheaper**." You have to be "**cheaper because...**" People generally need to think they know why the price is lower. It is especially effective for referral purposes if that reason appears to be something of an inside secret or at least not known by the general public.

All of this is achieved by managing peoples' perceptions. In most cases you are not going to do anything with your product or service, you are going to change how people think about it and how they talk to other people about it. This is important because in order for people to look good, they have to have some simple, plain message that they can convey quickly and eloquently.

> To look good, we need simple, plain messages that can convey quickly and eloquently.

If it is a very complicated distinction or if your product is very sophisticated and requires a lot of detailed information and I try to tell someone else about it and I stutter, stumble and fumble then I am not going to look good. That means I am not going to refer it again.

We need something that is very viral in character. A virus is one of the smallest living things there is and yet is one of the most prolific and successful. I think a virus is only four strands of DNA and barely even a living thing at all. It is thousand of times smaller than a grain of sand. In spite of all that it can traverse six continents in the span of half as many days and infect millions and millions of people. The pandemic of 1918 that is often forgotten because it occurred during World War I, killed as many as a hundred million people in 18 months. It was a very simple virus. It came and went and disappeared. Nobody knows what happened to it. It could be back any day. But I digress.

We want to think "virus" in referral marketing, something that is very tiny that moves around very quickly, a very simple message. Your message ideally should be simple and be able to fit on a button or a pencil or a business card. It is not something that takes 15 minutes or even 5 minutes to explain.

So what does all this mean? What do we do with these calculations and scores? What we know from multiple regression analysis is how much you have got to have to get high referral behavior.

Novelty	=	100%
Utility	=	100%
Dependability	=	100%
Economy	=	100%
Total Score	**=**	**400%**

As you can see the total possible score is 400% (which is almost impossible to get).

All you really need for viral behavior, for very, very high referral activity is 315%. Once you reach 315% you don't have to do hardly anything to sustain it. It carries itself on. This is the threshold number that gets you very high referral behavior. You have probably heard about or read the book "*Tipping Point*" that addresses threshold numbers. You fall much below 315% and the referral behavior is drastically reduced. We reliably modeled referral behavior and have proved 315% as the classic tipping point number for nearly every product or service.

What does that tell you? You cannot get to 315% with any three of the four drivers. You have to have a little bit of all four of them. It also means that even if you have the "best" product with 100% Utility, Dependability and Economy, if it does not have any Novelty, you cannot experience significant referral activity.

315% is the "tipping point" for viral behavior

Here are 3 important points about this mysterious number:

- A threshold number
- Close does not count for much
- Every point over delivers just incremental improvement

EXAMPLE:

315% = Total Score Necessary for Viral Referrals

	N = 60%	70%
	U = 80%	80%
	D = 100%	100%
	E = 60%	65%
	Total = 300%	**315%**
Referrals = 0.15 / customer		**1.00 / customer**
		600% Improvement!

It is a classic tipping point and literally 300% or 310% will give you only marginal viral behavior. Some of the benchmark numbers that we have discovered:

- A typical score for a lot of businesses or products would be about 300%. The resulting output behavior is about 0.15 per customer. In other words, for every 6 or 7 customers you would get 1 referral.
- When you get it up to 315% you might expect one referral for every customer. It is exponential. Every customer creates a new customer. So an added 15% on the N.U.D.E. model scale gives you 600% difference in terms of performance and referrals.

People ask me how does one ascertain the scores for the N.U.D.E. Model? There is a fairly complicated set of criteria and calculations. The working nature of my field (Social Network Analysis) is dry and complicated. I am not allowed to talk about it in moving vehicles for fear that the driver or pilot might be listening and go to sleep and everyone on board would be killed.

Even if you don't know what your N.U.D.E. score is, you know you have room for improvement. It is not critical that you know your exact score rather that you know how to add the needed points is what is critical.

315% =
Vroommmm!

You work with the drivers you naturally have and then build from the ones you are lacking. You can get to 315% easier than you think. It is just from not knowing that you miss the huge referral opportunities. It's one of those tipping points. When you get to 315% it is almost an audible acceleration (Vroommmm!), like the starting of a racecar. You will see more people in a day than you typically saw in a week when it really kicks in.

There are specific calculations of how we assess each one of those properties in detail but you can use simple ballpark assessments on a lot of these things. For example, you know if Utility is there but you don't know if the perception is there. There is a dynamic ratio between the real Utility and the perceived Utility, so a lot of what you are doing is managing and understanding the customer's perception of Utility. This is critical.

The thing that almost everyone believes is their product or services are useful. I have met very few people over the years committed to delivering a product or service that is useless. Well, maybe attorneys and a few MLM's but for the most part, most people believe they are delivering some value in the world, therefore, because they believe that, they cannot see how peoples' perceptions could be any different. That really screws them up. If people do not recognize the Utility then it will not get referred.

So, your score may be so close to 315% and attaining viral marketing. With just a little management of perceptions you could hit the tipping point and move yourself into the viral referral domain. But until you figure out what it would take to get you there, you will sputter along. You will get some referrals but not really experience viral behavior.

It is almost instantaneous when you find the best way to hit 315%. You can almost hear it go clunk, wham, when you hit the tipping point. When people hear your message as something that will make them look good, when they know exactly what they want to say about you, they become anxious to go out and tell their friends; it takes very little time at all. Now not everyone will engage in referral behavior but a lot of people will refer two and three and four people so it all balances out.

Let me back up a moment. I am speaking about one specific type of referral. Many people think that referrals are when someone gives you a name of a person for you to call. That is what we call a Class C referral; it is not really worth that much because they have not extended their personal credibility to endorse the product.

I am talking about Class A referrals where someone goes out and says: “Barry, I have got to tell you about this, you are going to love this, I can’t wait for you to try this and tell me about it!” That is a Class A referral. When I am talking about the one to one ratios from 315%, those are from Class A referrals. I don’t even keep track of the Class B or C referrals where somebody gives you a name or they send you to a website. I want only face-to-face personal endorsements because those are the most powerful, the most likely to get the results.

This why 315% is critical, even for those of you who have superlative products, to be able to express it in a way that people can communicate it. What you need for referral behavior to be sustained is people have to be able to represent the Novelty. In other words, you have to tell somebody why it is new and different.

How we communicate the Novelty is just as important as the Novelty itself. Because what we are basically looking to do here is help people look good. We’re trying to help people look smart by mentioning your product to someone else.

We have done this now with a lot of businesses to test the theory. I’ve actually used this with everyone from **A**ccountants to **Y**odelers (Well, it was actually just one yodeler down in Austin. I’m looking for a “**Z**” product but I haven’t found one yet). We have found that any type of business can apply this as long as they think about how they can represent themselves as novel.

Go for an Extraordinary Guarantee

There are a lot of different ways that constitute Novelty and also enhance Utility and Dependability. One of my favorite ways, if you've got the confidence and can afford to do this, is to offer an extraordinary guarantee of some type. The more extraordinary the guarantee … the more the Novelty.

In my particular case I guarantee certain results in retention agreements or I don't charge them a dime. That's a lot of Novelty, most consulting firms don't make that type of guarantee so that keeps it interesting enough for people to mention me to their peers and other organizations.

Simple things can create Novelty. We worked with a physician's office not long ago, and he was looking to increase his family business. He wanted more patients with children because they get sick a lot and increased business increases revenue. It's a money thing. The only Novelty we installed there was a big teddy bear, a five foot tall teddy bear and a digital camera. So, whenever people brought their kids in, they got their pictures taken with the big teddy bear. That wore off after a few months (the teddy bear didn't wear off, the Novelty wore off) and then we decided to let the kids play doctor with the teddy bear. We put a thumping speaker in the teddy bear's chest and let the kids listen to it with a stethoscope. That wore out after about six months and we added something else to it. This is a simple addition but guess how much his practice increased over the last year since the teddy bear was added? His business has tripled. He literally closed his practice and he is no longer taking new patients. The growth was almost exclusively from referrals.

The Novelty is what people pass along. It is what's unique, what they talk about when they say:

- this restaurant …

- that car wash…
- this consultant …

The Utility, Dependability and Economy are not mentioned but they are taken into consideration. What you have to ask yourself is "Do people appreciate your Utility, Dependability and Economy?" How do they know your Utility, Dependability and Economy? It varies a lot based on product. If we're talking about food – well everyone eats so you have instant Utility on some types of products.

Dependability is not as much an issue for other products. If you can't get it anywhere else, you're willing to take a chance with its Dependability. Each product and service has certain unique aspects but they all come into play. If people can't make an assessment of Dependability, they become hesitant.

Here's an example: If you went to a restaurant and it was absolutely outstanding twice but the 3rd time it was only mediocre, would you refer it to anyone? Nope. This is a really interesting part of the restaurant industry. This is what kills restaurants and why they are not able to sustain high referral activity over time. When you go to a restaurant the first time and there is huge Novelty, your attention is on the Novelty. "Wow, this is different, that's really cool, look at this menu!" The next time you go and it's familiar, you are no longer distracted by the Novelty, so any imperfections in the food quality, the service, the ambiance, or what ever, are more evident. We gave referred to this before but now I am going to say a bit more about how to deal with it.

> People avoid Novelty. They like the safety and comfort of the familiar.

There is a way to get past this and it's a big challenge for many new businesses besides restaurants. All new businesses naturally are candidates for referral behavior but if they don't take care of

Dependability, they lose the referral behavior really quickly. There is a way around that as well. We explore that later.

Most people avoid the Novelty because we like the safety and comfort of the familiar. Once we start doing something a particular way, we tend not to throw change-ups, we don't do things differently. But if we realized how important it is for people to want to refer us, we would start looking for ways to change our business all of the time. That is where referral business comes from.

I'll put my accountant hat back on for just a moment. Referral activity is the single most valuable asset a business can have. If you have your customers actively marketing for you, you cannot lose. I have never seen a business or product lose that has high referral activity. It's almost impossible for it to occur.

People always want to know how they can calculate their exact N.U.D.E. score and the answer is, you can't but you can get close simply by looking from the customer's perspective. Unfortunately, for many business owners this is difficult, if not impossible. They are simply standing too close, have too much invested and know too much about their product or service to be able to think as a new customer would.

It may help to ask a detached objective third party, someone who won't be too concerned about hurting your feelings. Even there, however, the most difficult attributes to assess are Utility and Dependability. No one wants to acknowledge his or her product or service as not needed or cannot be counted on. Keeping always in mind that these are perceptions is the challenge. Understanding that people will believe whatever they want unless deliberately and effectively directed to do otherwise is not easy to remember.

In general, try to lose any obsession with identifying your exact N.U.D.E. score and focus on where each respective perception comes from and understanding how to manage it. Take Utility for example, part of the trick here is recognizing that you are working to address a customer's perception regarding the needs and possible applications of your product or service for someone in their social network, not themselves.

If we take, as one possible example, a carpet cleaning service, most of the people in an average individual's network have carpeting somewhere in their home. The problem is you generally think of needing a carpet cleaning service when your carpet is dirty. Ordinarily that means you would have to be thinking of people with dirty carpet in order to see the Utility of referring a carpet cleaning service to them. That is kind of a problem to bring up politely in a conversation.

Imagine this referral:

> "*Mary, I was just noticing the condition of your carpet and wondering where you put all the livestock when I am at your house so I thought I would mention this great carpet cleaning service I use.*"

It is likely Mary's reply; if you are standing on her carpet will be something like:

> *"And do you know how they do with blood stains, especially your blood type?"*

You see there are some instances where the Utility is present in reality but not as a perception simply because we do not want to hurt someone's feelings or upset them in any way. There is no Utility inside an embarrassing conversation.

What can you do? In this case, the carpet cleaning service might try to de-emphasize the cleaning aspect and focus on other useful attributes. By calling attention to their love for pets and pet owners, as an example, we use chemicals that are pet-friendly and pet-conscious. Our products leave no offensive residue or odor for even the most sensitive canine and kitty noses. Then the referring parties, aware of the Utility, might go to their friends who have pets. Another example for the carpet cleaner might be emphasizing how well they handle large or expensive furniture. Then you would think of the Utility for friends with a lot of furniture. Are you starting to see how the perception of Utility works?

For a carpet cleaning service, this is critical because they will have to work very hard to achieve a Novelty score of even 20% or 30%. That means they have to be nearly spot on perfect (pun intended) on Utility, Dependability and Economy in order for them to reach the magic 315% threshold.

Backing into Your N.U.D.E. Number

For some businesses it would be simple to arrive at a close approximation of their N.U.D.E. score by calculating it from the results-end. What I mean is you will look at how many referrals you are getting (here again I am only talking about Class A referrals) and compare that to the known outcome from a given N.U.D.E. score.

Here is what I mean:

Referral Rate	NUDE Score	# of Existing Customers for 1 Referral
0.15	300%	1 referral / 6-7existing customers
0.10	290%	1 referral / 10 existing customers
0.05	250%	1 referral / 20 existing customers

Referral rates significantly below the range of 0.05 or a N.U.D.E. score of about 250% indicates you are in deep,

deep yogurt as far as referrals are concerned. These are just approximations but they give you an idea of your total score.

> "Good News
> &
> Bad News"

Of course you will want to know where you are strongest and where you are weakest. I would like to respond with the classic "Good News / Bad News." The bad news is you probably cannot determine exactly how each attribute scores. The good news is you do not really have to know the number. It is much simpler and more effective to first start looking at where you can add points.

Balance, Rolling the Diads

So let's look at one of the challenges. A lot of things in mental models, the way we calculate things exist in what we call diametric juxtaposition (because people in my field like to talk like that). We will call these diads. A diad is a balancing act. There is usually a balancing act between Novelty and Utility.

Novelty ←→ Utility

Here's why: if something is highly useful then the chances are it already exists and it is in a fairly common form. If it is very, very high Utility then it almost always sacrifices on the Novelty side. Said in another way, it is very hard to have high Novelty without compromising Utility.

On the other hand, if something is extremely unusual and unfamiliar, there may not be a perceived need for it. No one has had it before. Now sometimes that can work both ways. Sometimes in the history of market research there have been some notorious snafus. When the market research was done for ATM's, before they were out on the market, nobody wanted them. There was absolutely no interest in ATM's. "Why wouldn't I have a teller take care of me that already knows me?" VCR's were the same way, "why would I want to watch a TV show later?" Answering machines were another one, "why would I want to answer the phone when I'm not home?"

So, generally speaking when something is really unfamiliar, so novel that we don't even have a context for it; we do not see the usefulness of it. Some of you have products that are like that. The perception you have to manage is the Utility. You have to make it clear how it will be useful. You have to be vivid, specific and clear about how this product will change your life in some important way because if you don't do that the Novelty alone will actually hurt you.

The stand-alone Novelty, particularly when it is over-the-top, unfamiliar, never-heard-of-before Novelty, has to be balanced with Utility. We are always trying to manage that perception, that ratio so that people can see that even though they can't imagine what this is like, it would be useful.

An interesting thing is that people will buy things and wonder why they bought it. When you ask people about salad shooters. *"Oh, I must have one because it is so simple and I will eat healthier!"* Go to any city in America, you will find 500 salad-shooters in garage sales on any given weekend. We saw the Utility and there was Novelty but in fact these things are pointless. Obviously market research is not always reliable on things like this.

So, when it is really novel, people cannot always see the use for it. Conversely, if it has very high Utility, it has probably already been invented. It is a big balancing act.

Let's talk about the second diad. Dependability and Economy are always in balance. Let's look at a product or service that does something a lot cheaper such as a piece of exercise equipment that does the work of 3 other pieces of equipment or a health supplement that does what 4 others do; people are going to be a little bit suspicious of that. Everyone thinks that it cannot be as good as it claims even though they have a lot of experience that things like that can be effective.

Dependability ←→ Economy

> You must manage the perception!

It is always a matter of managing that perception. If it is too inexpensive or it is too economical then we tend to suspect it's reliability and then we make that worse by giving a money-back guarantee. If you understand the diads, it is easier for you to start to manage the mental model that people need to form, in order to see your business as a good candidate for referral behavior.

The balancing act between Dependability and Economy is like the old "good-fast-cheap" decision matrix. Where you pick any two: good, fast, or cheap. Many people believe that if it is very Dependable it is probably expensive. If it is the cheapest, it is usually not dependable. Now is that true? No, but it is the way people build their mental model. What you have to remember is that perception is reality for most people. The way people choose to think about it, the way people recognize the attributes is going to determine whether they will look good when referring it to someone else.

What we are doing here is managing perception. None of this is real. These are the images, the decisions that people are forming unconsciously in their mind. These are the calculations that we are doing unconsciously at billions of calculations per second in some cases. All we need to know is how to manage those calculations. How do we get people to form the correct assessment?

Now the great news is most of you in your business propositions and business models have at least two of the four drivers built in at a very high level. Many of you have three out of four. So all you have to do is get whatever that missing item is to work. All you have to do is push the total score over 315% and you are there.

When people start thinking of you as having Novelty, Utility, Dependability and Economy in the appropriate ratio, at the appropriate level then they start recommending you. Why? It will make them look good. It will enhance their standing.

> It is simply a perception

Here is one cautionary note regarding Dependability. Many people but certainly not all make a default inference that complexity automatically compromises Dependability. Not that this is true. It is a sort of background assumption many people have. As one example of how people sometimes shoot themselves in the foot in regards to this principle is by calling something a "system" that does not need to be. Calling it a system can work against you on Dependability and Economy. For many people, it sounds both more complicated therefore less dependable and at the same time more expensive.

If it does not have to be described as a system, you generally want to avoid that word. Once more, for the record, this is simply a perception. It is not the truth.

The Results are What Count

Most of us don't realize how much our words impact everything. You must design what you say about your products or services carefully. Often people want to explain how the product works or why it is so effective. This is very often a mistake. What really get people's attention are the results.

> Nobody gives a crap about process.
> It is the results that get people's attention!

You have really got to talk to people about the money they would save or the time they would save. You may even have a product or service that is a process. Remember what I say about process? **Nobody gives a crap about process.** You have to talk to the customer about the results.

What are three big results your product provides that the customer will be excited about, that they will want to tell other people about? You have to be specific and tell how much, how many, and what results. You can give averages, you may have to do some research. This is your sizzle, your Novelty.

Breakthrough in the N.U.D.E. Model

Add to all of these calculations we have to consider the "TANSTAAFL Paradox." We have heard all of our lives and most of us believe whole-heartedly that

"**T**here **A**in't **N**o **S**uch **T**hing
As **A** **F**ree **L**unch"

This has been called the TANSTAAFL Paradox. If someone tells you they have a product that will eliminate all Spam and reduce your email handling time by 90%, you are automatically skeptical, are you not? It sounds too good to be true, right? And what is the truth about things that seem too good to be true? Exactly.

People with breakthrough products or services are always confronting the TANSTAAFL Paradox. Here is another Good News/Bad News scenario. The good news is that referrals are an excellent strategy for climbing out of the TRANSTAAFL trap. If someone you know and trust tells you the product actually does perform as promised, you are generally much more willing to suspend your disbelief.

The bad news is that the "looking good" imperative may keep us from mentioning an extraordinary product or service because the referring party is both reluctant to confront the likely skepticism and unwilling to risk their credibility unless the product or service is believed to be 100% reliable. There is nothing more embarrassing than making an over-the-top endorsement and then having it fail to meet the referred parties expectations.

If we refer the breakthrough product or service and it works, we look great. But on the downside, if it does not, we are the goats. What generally happens in this case is we will refer the breakthrough product or service to someone whose esteem we are more willing to risk.

To summarize the problem with breakthrough products or services you have what could be described as literally, Toxic Novelty. Something so new and unfamiliar that it is literally frightening to be among the first to adopt it. Secondly, you automatically have somewhat questionable Utility because almost no one has used it yet. The perception of Dependability is almost invariably going to be low because there is little or no track record. Compounding all of this, the Economy of something so unproven is always suspect. It could be a total waste of time.

It is becoming clearer through all of this why it is so difficult to bring really revolutionary products to market successfully. But wait – it gets worse. Traditionally there is a group that seeks out these types of products or services who, in fact, gain a substantial portion of their identity from doing so. These are the infamous "early adopters." These folks will try anything so long as it is new.

Here is more Good News/Bad News. The good news is that makes them likely customers for the breakthrough products or services. The bad news is they often have little credibility when referring products to anyone other than fellow "early adopters." That is because these guys (and they are in fact almost all guys) are known for trying things just because they are new, not because they are good or useful. This may help to explain to some degree why the first customers for many products or services wind up being the only customers.

This may seem pretty grim if you have a breakthrough product or service but I am a long time subscriber to the engineering axiom that says: *"any problem well stated is half solved."* Now that we have painted the target as they say in the military, let's get to work beating the TANSTAAFL Paradox.

By the way, if you happen to have anything to do with change implementation in corporations, you may find several elements of this conversation helpful in overcoming resistance to change in your organization. The TANSTAAFL Paradox cripples many well-designed initiatives.

What to do with TANSTAAFL?

Here is one trick for handling TANSTAAFL. Although it is no longer politically correct, there was a relatively common expression around the time my

Dad was a boy that said: *"every cripple finds his own way of walking."* I have always found that phrase both poignant and poetic in many ways. As someone who has gotten along with a severe hearing impairment most of my adult life, I have had to find ways to get along in a hearing world. That not only does not make me stand out but also even allows me to provide insight and perspective not easily available to those with normal hearing.

Essentially I have made my handicap into an asset. Now I was fortunate enough to be given a disability, not of my choosing certainly and if I were offered normal hearing back today, I would probably take it but I would never surrender the experience and perspective it has provided me.

But what you may ask, does all this have to do with overcoming the TANSTAAFL Paradox? It is quite simple really. I expect some of you might have figured it out already. That is right, I want you to cripple yourself. Of course, not literally and of course, not you rather your product or service. Breakthrough products and services, in order to be perceived as credible desperately need a handicap to offset the too-good-to-be-true Toxic Novelty.

The question is how to expose that handicap to the market. If you simply tell them about it outright such as "I have to admit it does emit just a smidge of deadly sterilizing radiation," it will sound almost like false modesty. The concept you need to be acquainted with is a close cousin to "De Ja Vu." In French, "De Ja Vu" means: "seen before." There is an equally valuable and intriguing experience called "Pres Que Vu" which means "almost seen" and that is exactly how we want your breakthrough product's hidden handicap to appear to your market.

> "Looking Good" is the bottom line!

It is something that is just noticed out of the corner of their eye not really hidden but unnoticed by the casual observer. Ideally, all early customers will believe that they are the only ones to have noticed this subtle flaw. We are now naturally situated for high referrals.

It always comes back to the looking good imperative. Having discovered your weakness, your Achilles heal, almost anyone will be excited to refer your product / service because they will also be sharing the inside secret that keeps it from being a free lunch. We are talking about Brinkmanship here, taking something to the very edge of "too good to be true" and causing it to hang there as if by magic in that perfect market position – "<u>almost</u> too good to be true." Managing the "almost" part of that is the critical secret to aligning Breakthrough Products/Services with the N.U.D.E. model.

SECTION THREE

REFERRAL BEHAVIORS

What are Referral Behaviors?

Now I want you to look for a moment at the last time you referred anything to anybody. It could be a book, a movie, a restaurant or anything. Ideally it would be a product or a service. Think of a product or a service where you don't have any financial advantage from promoting it. Why did you do that? Which of the drivers did it have?

In many cases to help people understand this model clearly, I ask people to share experiences from their lives where they have referred things to someone else. Then we look and see which of the properties were clearly present. We will share a few of those with you so you can start to see how the referral model works in your own experience.

> You can tell anyone anything as long as it is about someone else

One of the most valuable things I have learned in my consulting career is you can tell anybody anything as long as it is about someone else.

Keep in mind this is the easy part. We are looking for when the referral attributes are present. The more important and difficult trick is recognizing when they are not present.

Here are some examples of referral behaviors that people commonly ask about:

- **Challenging Referrals:** Consultants, particularly business consultants and coaches, are challenged on almost all four axes in the N.U.D.E. Model. This is just the truth. There is not much clear Novelty. People are not clear about the use for them, they are not always dependable, and compared to doing nothing (which is what a lot of people are doing) they are not that economical. So, you have got to work all four drivers. You've got to really attend to those things before people will really see you as a candidate for referral behavior.

Now, here's the good news. You can do that. You just have to be very clear and specific about those four drivers. Actually, in your case, you want to work the last three, because in consulting and in coaching, if you can demonstrate your Dependability, Utility and Economy; that constitutes Novelty itself. You have to talk to people, give them your results, give them the numbers that you produced, show them your Utility, Dependability and Economy. Set them up to see what you offer. The question that people have about coaches and consultants is "how do I know?" Be clear and specific, offer any details and that should take care of it for you.

For me, I am technically a consultant. I don't like to use that term. I say Social Network Analyst or Subject Matter Expert. You know the old joke:

> *"A consultant is someone who can tell you 100 ways to make love but you can't help noticing he doesn't ever have his own girlfriend."*

That is the sort of impression consultants have made in many organizations. In health care, for example, consultants came through health care about 10 years ago and dropped this Managed Care bomb on them and today the health care workers that are left will pretty much spit on you if they think you are any form of a consultant. So, it's a hard world out there for consultants because people have not done the best jobs or delivered in the past.

The good news is people love discovering and referring good coaching and consultants.

- **Requested Referrals:** *"I referred an auto mechanic to a friend of mine. I suppose I did it to look good."* It definitely had Dependability and Utility. It didn't really need Novelty because she had already asked for it. So it's a little different because it was a requested referral.

In many cases attributes do double duty. This is one of those cases wherein Dependability and Economy insofar as auto mechanics are concerned also constitutes Novelty. I think Tom and Ray Magliozzi, the Car Talk guys, will bear me out on this. Clearly the Utility was there because there was the stated need for a mechanic.

It is also worth noting that in the case of requested referrals (i.e.: do you know a good realtor, doctor, attorney, etc.?). Novelty is less critical but Dependability is paramount.

- **Looking Good Referrals**: Vacation destinations are another common referral topic. This is such a thinly veiled effort to look good it almost doesn't count as a referral but let's talk about it anyway. We are generally more excited to talk about a vacation if it was to some place new, exciting and/or unfamiliar. It is only better if it is somehow exclusive.

If we talk about our trip to the Grand Canyon or Disney World to anyone other than immediate family and friends, it is usually to share some inside secret, unusual tip or information about a special deal. That is because generally speaking we assume quite a few people have already been there. In most cases where we go to a place that is a quite common vacation destination, we may only share about it with people who are less well traveled.

But the much more likely vacation referral, the primary reason many people travel is to be able to tell someone about an exotic destination where few people have been such as: Tanzania, Mustique, or the Ukraine. Although there is not a great deal of conventional Utility in visiting these far away or exotic destinations and equally little Economy for most of them. In most respects, they may be far less dependable except for this simple basic fact: when you recognize it is all to look good. The Novelty of discovering or being the first to visit a new destination has enormous Utility for our ego.

It is also very Dependable that people will at least be interested and more often fascinated by our visits to these unusual locals. As for Economy, how much are you willing to spend for people to be envious of you or fascinated by you.

- **Outcome-driven Referrals -** I talked with a client who has a watercolor journaling business, teaching people how to draw and paint what is happening in their lives. What do you think is my first question? What are the results? What do you produce for people? We are so fascinated by our processes. I am in love with the processes I use. I would love to talk about LaPlace Equations and Fourier Transforms but, as fascinating as I find it, I know that you all do not care. You just care about the results for you. Okay, now what are the results you produce with journaling? Be specific, be descriptive, be evocative; how does it make me feel good?

You may want to use illustrations. Some people when they are dealing with art. Art and music are exceptions where illustrations are often the best vehicle. Could you show me someone's art when they started your process and then someone's illustrations after 6 months? If you had a montage of those, that might be the best thing for you to do, then have people describing what was their mood, their experience, etc. when they started journaling and now. Use people's endorsements on that because this is a very personal experience. This is not something that everyone will get the same way. It is very unique and individualized. So you want to get individualized experiences displayed as clearly and distinctly as possible.

- **Tangible Reminders** - Some of you are going to have a hard time finding something to represent your product perfectly. There are a lot of things you can give people that create an opportunity for them to have a conversation about you or your product or service. There are a lot of things that are very simple and inexpensive that you can hand people that will sit on their desk or in their pocket or be in their car that give them an opportunity to broach the conversation. People are not, by and large, very good at starting conversations but once they are started they can carry them. One of the things that I would like to suggest is to give people things they can pass along that have messages on them.

For example, a pencil in the shape of a dollar sign, it is very simple but it has an underlying gimmick to it. This is a $28 pencil. It is made from recycled ground-up currency. $28 worth of recycled currency goes into each one of these pencils. It has a good message surface.

There are lots and lots of promotional products like pens. I had a doctor client whose patient load was about half what he wanted. He did not feel like he had any money to spend on marketing. We got him some very inexpensive pens and we printed on them the following:

Please take care of your health
Bring this pen back to Dr. Smith for a free new patient physical - (888) 888-1111

We printed 300 of those pens and handed them out to 300 patients. Within a matter of a month, he had so many new patients coming in from these pens that he could not see them all. Also, he got the pens back so he could hand them out again. Some of those pens were recycled 7 or 8 times. Some of them kept coming back, even if they were broken and out of ink.

Don't under estimate the power of a very simple representation. There are lots of products that will work like this. What you need to look for is something with a lot of printable surface and the message that people identify with. You need to use your imagination. You need to think "what would get my product out there in a favorable light, in a way that people will pass it on to their friends." Because, keep in mind, why do people refer things? They do it to look good! If I can give you something fun or handy or useful that you can then keep and give to other people. Tangible, physical representations improve the cycling of referrals by at least 30-40%. Sometimes lots more if you find the right product.

Get N.U.D.E. with Referral Behaviors

You need to have as comprehensive an understanding of this as you can. There is no trick to these referral behaviors. I want you to finish this book with the ability to apply this so you can use it immediately in your business model.

Let's look at it another way. Find a time where you would not refer something. When you liked something but you stopped. You could have recommended it but you didn't. I'll give you a hint, this happens all the times with restaurants. You like the restaurant. You know the people you could refer live in the area. It was reasonably priced. Why didn't you recommend it?

Generally the reason restaurants lose their referral base is Dependability. What happens all the time with restaurants is it is new and fresh and high Novelty. You are looking at the interesting décor, the menu is unique or whatever and you do not notice much about the service. You are not really conscious. You are not focused on the service or even the meal quality. You are all caught up in how different or unique it is.

Then the second time you go to the restaurant the Novelty is not as prominent. You have already seen this before. So now that you are not distracted by the Novelty, you notice the waiter was a little slow, there was a smudge on the glass, you had to wait a long time for the check and other Dependability issues become obvious. The perception of Dependability substantially affects our referral behavior.

Can you start to see how you are factoring these decisions in, making these calculations all the time in deciding what to refer? It is very easy for something to miss out because there is just one way to win, by reaching the tipping point of 315%, but lots of ways to lose.

- If you think they have already heard of it, you won't recommend it.
- If you think they may not need it, you won't recommend it.
- If you think it is not reliable, you won't recommend it.
- If you don't perceive it provides value, you won't recommend it.

So, it looks like it is pretty hard to get referrals. Generally speaking, most people are not maximizing their referrals because they don't know how to manage these properties, they don't know how to have people make the calculations in their favor.

> You have to take action to produce bigger results.

Look and see how you think you are doing in your business model. If you think you have 3 of the 4 drivers, how can you add the 4th one so you can make it to 315%?

Now let's look at some business examples. These are some clients who have missing drivers and we want to identify ways to add them.

Creating Novelty

Many of them will have Utility, Dependability and Economy down and what they are missing is Novelty. Some businesses have a really hard time with Novelty.

One physician in general practice has found that prescribing anti-depressants is one thing he does more and more. This is not something people automatically go out and recommend. Hey I've been down and now I'm taking pills to make me happy. So, we added some Novelty. The doctor bought a case of silly string and he added that to his prescriptions, telling the patients that if they haven't opened the can in a week or if they've used up 5 cans of Silly String in a week, they should come in so we can adjust the anti-depressant dosage. People were taking their Silly String to work and pointing out that their doctor had written a prescription for it. Within a week, there were over 20 referrals. Those Silly Strings price out at about 62 cents and a new patient is estimated to bring in about $2,850. That's a very good investment.

Anywhere you are looking for Novelty, you can find it if you get creative enough. Let's look at some examples of people who needed some Novelty.

Example 1 - Someone who owned a business that designed, installed and refurbished countertops is looking for Novelty. He has Utility. You need countertops or things will fall through and break. Dependability is there. As far as Economy, he was competitively priced. Let's say his total N.U.D.E. score is 270%. So he needs at least 45 points of Novelty. He needs something a little bit different. You could throw in the backsplash but we don't want to eat into his profits when we add the Novelty. We want to distinguish the company from the competition. The contracting industry tends to run over on deadlines so by offering an extraordinary guarantee, it might make a difference. If there is a promise to finish this order in 2 weeks (building in a little wiggle room for completion) or the company will "eat a bug" or refund 50% or something.

An extraordinary guarantee is like *"we will refund your money or your deposit or something and you still keep the goods."* You really have to put some skin in the game. The thing about extraordinary guarantees is they will make you better. They really force you to step up your game but people are impressed with it. It really adds to your Dependability too. And it is something people will tell other people about. Now if you are not willing to take on this sort of Novelty, then keep looking for something else.

Consider the customer experience when creating Novelty. If you are getting your existing counter tops replaced, your kitchen is probably a wreck for several days or weeks. What are you <u>not</u> doing? Cooking. What could you do for the customer that would constitute Novelty while addressing this lifestyle disruption? For one thing you could contact a "Home Meal Replacement" company that prepares delicious meals to microwave at their convenience. To offer a free dinner or two as a way of promoting their business or if no one was forward thinking enough for that, you could just find someone who was at least smart enough to sell them to you at their cost. Alternately, you could go to neighborhood restaurants (especially new ones) and ask for some substantial "remodeling refugee" discounts.

There are so many ways of creating Novelty once you get the hang of it. I share ideas like this for free when I speak to groups. I can do it for hours with all kinds of businesses and it's really fun but I'm not doing it to show off or just for my amusement. It is so that people can start to realize they can do it for themselves or maybe if not for themselves, they can at least do it for others. By the time I have created samples of Novelty for 10 to 15 businesses, I ask the audience to start participating to share how they see the perception of Novelty could be enhanced. It is a great exercise because it gets people thinking from a new perspective.

People really start to appreciate that the perception of Novelty is laying around waiting for their imagination to pick up and turn it into waves of new business.

Everything works better when you give people choices. So, to use the countertop guy as an example, you might offer a coffee maker, a toaster or a blender. You could even add: *"if we are late in delivering your product, you can have all 3."* What that does for you is everyone that comes into the customer's kitchen admires the nice coffee maker or blender and the customer says *"Oh, I got that with the countertops."* You want something that is tangible and easy to reference. You want them to tell somebody about this in order for you to get the benefit.

So that means it has to be fairly simple. I can't look stupid trying to explain how I got all these enhancements and tweaks and bells and whistles because it gets complicated real quick. There is a reason that the virus is one of the successful organisms on earth. It is really small and it is really simple. Most of your messages need to communicate in as few words as possible.

Keep in mind that countertops are not an easy one. They don't just scream Novelty.

Example 2 – There is a carpet cleaning company who, at the end of the job, gives the woman of the house a red rose. "Gimme's" are a nice touch. Now, I'm not saying you always have to buy Novelty but if it is something that you have thought through, it will make a huge difference. Because legal issues can be very stressful, several of our attorney clients have offered either a relaxation CD, a session with a massage therapist, or massage cream to relieve stress in your back. These products have a good imprintable surface so you can remind them who contributed to their relaxation. You see it is not that hard to make an attorney look thoughtful, it is just surprising which makes it novel.

Example 3 - There was a client with a new type of tool organizer called Tools Away™. To begin with, on a scale of one to ten, using myself as an example, consider tool organizer versus behavioral statistician, which is more boring? It is hard to say. I'm sorry but Novelty in that context is limited. It may make a couple of clutterers' faces light up but mostly it is not something people want to tell other people about. You may have a product or service as exciting as this.

> There are 3 distinct types of customers

The hardest part of Novelty for most people is distinguishing who is the actual customer. You may not have thought about this but you need to. There are three distinct types of customers with important sub-species.

They are rarely all the same person. They can, of course, each derive satisfaction from referring you.

1. **Economic Buyer** - The simplest and most commonly understood customer is the Economic Buyer. Plainly enough they are the person who completes the transaction by paying for the product. This does not necessarily imply that they were the decision maker.

2. **Decision Maker**- the decision maker is actually the person most likely to engage in referral behavior. This is because they are the person who can take credit for the wisdom and foresight to have chosen the product.

    a. **Influencer** - A barely separate sub-species of the Decision Maker is the Influencer. Women and children are master Influencers. The Influencer contributes as much to the final decision as all the other factors combined. This person will also seek to undermine the acceptance or success of any choice other than his/her own.

    b. **Clueless Agents** - To the degree that men may constitute a second sub-species that we could call arrogantly deluded Decision Makers or perhaps more accurately Clueless Agents for those they believe to be less powerful than themselves.

3. **End-User** – The third type of customer is the End-User. They may not have purchased the product or even have chosen it but they are the one who primarily benefits from it. End-Users are the most

likely ones to be the referring party. They are also, generally, the most credible referring party, inasmuch as they have direct experience of it.

Why am I telling you this now? Regarding the tool organizer, it is critical to be able to establish Novelty, to understand clearly and specifically which one is your real customer. In the case of Tools Away™ it might be easiest to assume that the customer is the End-User. Therefore predominantly men interested in squaring away their garage or tool shed. If this were the case you would appeal to their practical and analytical side and suggest they would never lose or damage another tool or that their tools would never wind up in some jumbled, impossible-to-separate pile.

It is not so much that these ideas are wrong as that they are ignorant of a basic fact. Tool organizers, or organizers of any kind, are more or less like greeting cards in that they are rarely purchased by heterosexual men except under duress.

Women, in this case, are both the Economic Buyer and the Decision Maker. So the Novelty has to be created from a woman's perspective. The Looking Good Message has to appeal clearly and simply to a female. Does that mean no one else will ever buy one of these or that a man couldn't buy one for himself? No, of course not. But looking from the perspective of referrals and considering who is most likely to recommend the product and to whom, we are smart to go with the odds.

Understanding this tells us not only how to get more referrals but where and how to sell the product to begin with. The logical place to sell such a product might seem to be hardware stores or garden centers, and no doubt some will be sold there. The less obvious hot spot would be places such as craft shows garden shows or even grocery and drug stores. Catalogues would be great too. Why? These are all places where women shop.

What do you say to engage them in the idea? How about something like: *"he'll thank you for it later."* This is a kernel of a "**Looking Good Message (LGM)**" which we discuss at length in Section Four.

Example 4 - Wholesale furniture company – How do I use referral marketing when my customers are retailers and design firms and they are competitive against each other? This is a tough one and many of you are in similar situations. You have very loosely networked groups of customers who don't talk to each other very often. Basically, for this purpose, your network is not the dealer it is the end-users.

The end-users who actually buy the furniture from the retailers are your only opportunity for referrals. Because generally speaking, when your customers are competing, they will not refer a good product to each other. It would be like cutting their own throats.

So the thing that you have to find is a way for people to talk about your product that says why they like it better or what is different about it What would you say would be the most distinctive aspect of your furniture that sets it apart from other furniture of its type?

This is very important to create Novelty because this one has Utility, Dependability and Economy. The usefulness of the product is the prestige that someone gets when they have this furniture in their home.

For some people there is a tag line, some little resident expression such as "*if Feng Shui built furniture, this is what it would look like or maybe this furniture makes you want to sit outside naked.*" There is something you could say that encapsulates what your furniture is about that constitutes your unique selling proposition or tag line but you have got to set yourself apart so that people can say it.

It is a difficult thing to remember that people have to be able to look good when they tell someone about it. It has got to be something evocative, something that expresses it clearly.

Tangible representations are also valuable in increasing Novelty when you have a really great product. One of the best things you can do is come up with a model of the product. For example, if you had little tiny teakwood models that held business cards that people could pass along. Find something that clearly represents the product and something that can be handed to someone else. Physical representations are sometimes the only way to get across the Novelty, because it is visual.

Example 5 - How about marketing a video email product? Candidly, this is one of those things that until you get a video email, you are probably not going to be interested in sending one. So the thing you have to do is get people to look at it first. This is an example of what we call "**Invisible Novelty**." Nobody has seen it because it's so new. You have got to get it out there through some mode, some broadcast. Get some high volume user to get some out there. While the Novelty is nearly 100%, it doesn't count for much because nobody has seen it. That's over the top, actually. Novelty is trumped, or cancelled out, by outright weirdness.

Now once people have seen it, you are a great candidate but your challenge is getting it out there in front of people. Some things have taken off on the Internet. Some games have been sold on the Internet and people refer those around everywhere quick. There are some particular demographics at play there. There's one other challenge – 95% of referral activity takes place face to face. There's a reason for this. Since we give referrals to look good, we want to see their faces when we make the referrals. If you are trying to make something work virally, through Internet or telephone, it's not as likely to occur that way. Generally, it's local social networks that make the difference.

Example 6 - We had an artist breaking into landscape photography who asked: *"how do I develop referrals?"* In art, the referral model is usually about introducing people to something that they have not seen or heard of before. Only a few people actually engage in referrals of traditional artists of any type (including music, painting, sculpture, etc.). They are people who have a particular interest in that type of activity. It gives them pleasure to introduce people to new media or new artists. That network is usually fairly easy to locate. They are the people who will go to movies; subscribe to related magazines, etc. They can be very, very active referrers, unfortunately often without very much productivity.

When someone comes and tells me about a new sculpture show in Dallas, I probably won't go because I am just not into that. I'm from Oklahoma and I'm not that classy. After all, we were admitted to the Union in 1907 so Arkansas would have somewhere to make fun of. Anyway, my point is that art referrals are a special case.

The way most referrals occur in art is that someone will take you to see the show. Here's the problem, we are into a descriptive issue, unless I have a sample of the art and someway to show someone, it's very difficult to look good by telling someone about something that is visual. So, I may be very excited about it as an art fan (which I'm not) and I may tell a lot of people about it but I can't really describe it effectively enough to get them engaged with it. I can't really describe it effectively in a way that I really look good. So, unless they have some sample of the art or music, it's really difficult. Postcards, tee shirts, note cards, etc. are very effective.

Of course, if I'm conversant in that world and can reference the artist in some more sophisticated context such as saying *"he is like a young Degas channeling a mature Modigliani."* It might make me sound very clever and aware (or maybe even snobby) but it would not necessarily heighten your interest because you might have no idea what I was saying unless of course you are a fellow art snob.

Creating Utility

I want to discuss if Utility were not present, because if it isn't perceivable you are never going to reach 315%.

Example 7 - There is a woman who owns a private investigation service. Her methodology is very sophisticated and can serve as Novelty but on the other side of the diad, people can't see how to use it. Her clients don't understand how many varied things she can do for them.

Part of her problem is that her Utility is actually risk avoidance. It is safety. Because safety is not a familiar deliberate purpose, they don't see the Utility. It is kind of like insurance; people don't buy it because they want to. They buy it because they are supposed to have insurance.

You have to find some other way to convey the Utility. In a lot of cases the Utility is going to be recognizing the feeling that they get when they do it. Sometimes you have to give one away. In sales it is called a "puppy dog close". You put it in their hands and they say *"oh, it's a puppy dog, isn't he cute*" and they can't give it back. When you are having a hard time conveying Utility for people, the thing to do is to give them a free sample. Get them to try it. Give them a coupon to try it when they need it. Send out some coupons to clients (don't send them all at once so you aren't inundated) and then follow up with a phone call. Explain that you want them to try this other service you provide so they can see how valuable it is. That is how you might increase the Utility. That's not for everything but there is a way to establish Utility for almost everything.

Example 8 – A consultant was a specialist in spreadsheet and word processing software. She can show clients how to get maximum use out of their software by transferring tips through their cell phones. Products like that do really well when you give them away. Your biggest challenge is the Utility on that product. People don't see the immediate need for it. It's just like people didn't see the value of ATM's until they actually tried them. You are almost over the top in Novelty.

So, if you don't give people a clear use for the product (the Utility part of the diad) they won't be excited about it. You are going to have to give them the use of the product, or to show them a clear application that a lot of people would use it for. It has to be something that everyone would find value for if they thought about it. One way to balance the diad is to give them a piece of the product and have them use it and then offer them more of it for purchase.

Another way of establishing Utility is to use a simple analogy. Referencing something people are familiar with and feel they understand to describe something less familiar. For example: the software consultant could ask:

> *"What would it feel like driving your car in low gear and only being able to turn left? Obviously it would be very frustrating and take you a long time to get anywhere. What most people are doing with their software is just like that."*

This simple comparison might make it possible for them to understand the value (Utility) of what the consultant provides.

Another way of establishing Utility is by guaranteeing a particular result. In the case of the software consultant, it might be possible for her to explain clearly and specifically what will be different in the office as a result of her work:

- Will documents be error free?
- Will the time to generate documents be reduced by 20%, 30%, or more?
- Will client lists be 100% current?

These are all results that can be measured and clearly convey Utility.

Example 9 - One client asked about the N.U.D.E. model for the sale of his customized mattresses. Basically this product killed on all four of the drivers. It's a great candidate for huge referral activity. The only downside is the Utility because the buying cycle on mattresses is probably 5-10 years. The Utility window is the biggest handicap because normally people don't shop for mattresses unless they want to replace one because the old one is worn out. The Utility is "don't wait for the mattress to wear out because you can have a much better one than you thought you could." So, you have got to get past the ordinary Utility window, which is "replace it when it is dead."

This is true for a lot of businesses. Unless you have some way of demonstrating significant Utility, they are just going to wait until the life cycle of the product is met to get a new one. And then, they may not think of you when they are ready for replacement because 5 years is a long time to remember you. You have to keep emphasizing the upgrade, "how much better a mattress you can get than you thought you could." That's your Utility. The long product life cycle is your weakness in the referral model.

I would encourage you all to play this game with yourselves because the more you do it, the more you will be able to recognize the attributes; where you are light, where you are heavy and what you can capitalize on. Most of you, in terms of the candidate models (the way people form the mental model), are probably 250% to 285%. It wouldn't take that much work to have a referral based business. That's what I find over and over again with businesses. That extra 15-50 points you can eek out of 1, 2 or 3 new or alternative uses will put you over the top. But it is interesting because below 310%, or 300% you just don't get that much activity. It's one of those tipping points, because the mental model doesn't say *"hey, I'll look good (or smart or whatever) to tell somebody about this."*

Creating Dependability

When people are not sure that you, your products, or your services are not dependable, you have a problem. This is a tough one. This will kill your referrals if people don't recognize Dependability. If they are concerned in any degree, they will not refer you if they do not know you are reliable.

Dependability is the one attribute where most people do not realize they have a problem.

An extraordinary guarantee, in most businesses, is one of the simplest accesses to Novelty and it takes care of Utility and Dependability at the same time. There's a great book that is unfortunately out of print, by Christopher Hart called ***Extraordinary Guarantees*** with some classic examples of how companies have used these guarantees as a marketing slingshot.

Example 10 – There was a client who sold a unique and very credible nutritional supplement and people would discount it because they think it was just another one of "those" products. She had been broad-brushed. When she said supplement, people thought they knew what that was, so she was trapped in the opinions people have about supplements. It is not so much that her product is undependable as that the market for these types of products has been trained to be skeptical.

This is a case for an "extraordinary guarantee." Christopher Hart would suggest offering back twice their money or twice the supplement if it doesn't work. Now I caution you; you can only do this if it really does work. A simple money back guarantee is no longer effective because it is ordinary. But something bigger is more compelling. A double-back money back guarantee or twice the supplement until it works will put some skin in the game. You have to be able to take that risk. But it also tells the customer that you are willing to take that risk and still make money.

Example 11 – Creative services such as: advertising agencies, marketing consultants, graphic designers, etc. have problems measuring success and satisfaction. Here's something that I know works with creative types of organizations. This actually takes very little more effort than you are doing right now but the client satisfaction is considerably higher.

We are increasingly immersed in a menu-driven society. Everyone is using computers. You are always getting options. There are menus for everything. You always have a choice. So, people are increasingly expecting a choice. "***Good, better, best***" choices are the best ones to use in a creative environment. You don't tell them it is going to be "good, better, best." You tell them, "I'm not going to give you a design; I am going to give you three designs."

Most people are uncomfortable choosing from one single thing. That is why "time-share" presentations are so unpopular because it is "***take it or leave it***." But if you have a range of choices such as: A, B, or C. Most people will split the difference. They will weigh the choices and consider "C has too much of this," "A has less of that." Now they choose and feel like they have made an intelligent decision.

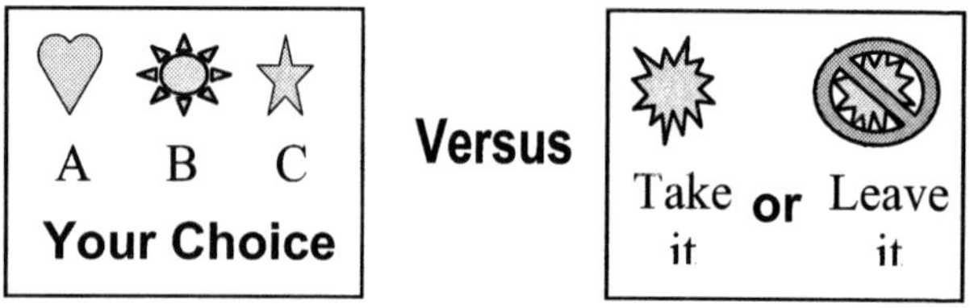

You have to help people feel comfortable. One of the things that make people feel concerned is when they feel uneasy. They think: *"I could screw up, I could make a mistake."* If you are choosing from a menu, A, B, or C; it is much easier to feel safe and comfortable, to make the appropriate decision, than if you have only one choice, *"take it or leave it."*

Many creative firms already offer a range of choices but they tend to be simple variations on a theme, more or less the same idea from slightly different angles or in different colors. What most creative types are unwilling to do is include one or more mediocre ideas so the perspective buyer will immediately be able to disqualify one and choose from the remainder.

It is surprising how confronting several great choices can be for many people. It is actually easier, and better, to give them the confidence to eliminate one option right away. You might think of it as priming the decision pump. The longer it takes for most of us to make a decision, the harder it gets. We tend to over think and consider too many variables, especially when we are in unfamiliar territory.

How is this related to Dependability? This is a hard thing for most creative people to get but most of their customers are not buying creativity, per se. What they are actually buying is the way they feel about being involved in the creative process. The Dependability comes in knowing they will get that feeling.

Example 12 - A client was targeting real estate professionals with a virtual office product. The referrals are from the real estate brokers. It's probably novel. Here's the challenge; in professional services, Dependability is usually assessed as a function of time and money. People take a *"wait and see"* attitude when you start something, even though it may be dependable, nobody wants to be the one to find out. Nobody wants to be first.

If you have some kind of testimonial it gives you some presumed Dependability. If someone has been using it for a year and they can say what great results the product is producing for them; that would really help the perceived Dependability. The other drivers are pretty strong. You can see where it would be an economic advantage to have that kind of service.

Your challenge to get into a good referral mod for this product and most professional services is Dependability. People are naturally skeptical because everyone makes big claims about how much difference they will make. You have to have some credible way of backing up those claims or they can do more harm than good.

If all you can say is that it has been tested on prisoners, it is really hard to have people refer it, particularly for things that impact people's careers. I work a lot with doctors and they don't like to be first, they don't like to take chances on things. This is their life that you are messing with and if it doesn't work, it's a problem.

Many companies attempt to overcome this resistance by offering a free trial period or much less effectively, a money back guarantee. In my experience neither of these approaches are especially effective when selling to a professional services environment.

A strategy we've used to good effect here to get a new or unfamiliar product into the market is the evaluation or beta approach. In this approach you are not asking someone to buy the product at all, you are asking for their expertise and more importantly their critical opinion in exchange for free use of the product. In some cases, it is even productive to offer a monetary incentive or other tangible reward in exchange for their participation.

Obviously enough when it comes time to debrief on the product, it just makes sense to ask them if they would like to continue using it for a nicely discounted price. If you are paying attention you may be wondering how this enhances the perception of Dependability?

In our experience, as best we can tell, it does a couple of things. First, it invites people to be critical and look for flaws that can then be addressed. Secondly, it shows your concern for receiving expert inside advice. Lastly, it shows what a discerning individual you are in recognizing their expertise and that makes them feel good which is never a bad idea.

Example 13 – One unique idea was a drive-thru nail salon. It is an unusual concept and the key is leveraging the Novelty. Obviously, it is 100% in the Novelty department. If you were in a hurry to get your nails done the Utility would be fairly high. Dependability might be a challenge during busy hours when the line gets too deep. Here's the thing, people will sacrifice some Dependability for convenience. That's one of the only big trade off's. People in a hurry will take a chance that something won't work. People are most likely to take a risk when they are in a hurry (don't ask me why). For this concept to work, <u>everything</u> would depend on speed and convenience. If it ever took longer than it would to walk in to a conventional nail salon, both the Novelty and Dependability would be immediately lost.

Of course, it should be apparent, that if the product is essentially convenience, ease or speed that is what must be delivered dependably. We know nearly everything in a convenience store costs more than it would at a grocery store. If we are in a hurry, that cost is acceptable, so long as it does not take any longer than we expect. I am not saying many people are likely to refer a convenience store but if you are a business where convenience, ease, and/or speed are a big part of your selling proposition; you want to be very accountable for people's perceptions of those factors.

For example, if you say you are the fastest, that does not readily translate into a referable characteristic. There is nothing you can hang your hat on there, so to speak. Any assertion regarding speed generally needs to include some specific temporal increment and a confirmation. Be as explicit as possible, a guaranteed one-day turnaround is good but 24-hour turnaround is better. As a general example:

> *"You brought your car / dry cleaning / etc. in at 8:30 AM yesterday and we did not have it ready for you until 9:00 AM today. We apologize and here is a coupon for 25% off your next visit."*

That clearly shows you are committed to being dependably fast and in the right business that can make you very referable.

Creating Economy

Economy can be one of the most challenging attributes from which to manage people's perceptions. How do you know if they will consider it a good value, if it has a favorable effort to outcome ratio? Generally, people assess value based on known alternatives. With familiar products or services, it can be as simple as knowing how the price or quality companies. Bear in mind that quality can be very much a part of the Economy assessment.

The perception of quality is readily manageable in a number of ways. The packaging, the setting, the presentation, the general context in which the product or service is delivered can all influence the perception of quality.

- The ideal perception for optimal referrals, in terms of Economy, is that you are getting more for less.
- The second best perception is that you are getting more for the same money or effort.
- The third condition in which Economy still qualifies for referrals is that you are getting the absolute best of something no matter what price.

Example 14 – There was a Human Resource Strategist who was having difficulty marketing to small businesses and start up companies. The difficulty in marketing to small businesses is basically unless there is a clear return on investment, it is difficult to compel the sale. Unless they've had some kind of a catastrophic failure that causes them to lose money, they are not motivated. You have got to work some results or numbers that they are in danger of losing. Unfortunately, scaring them is needed in remedial products (something that is designed to fix something).

You depend on something being broken in order for you to come in and do your work so you have to use FUD (fear, uncertainty and doubt) to get their attention. That is your Utility. You have fairly good Novelty because you are one of a few doing this. You have a good track record so you have Dependability. Therefore, you have to work on Utility and Economy. And you can do those pretty much in the same sentence; *"we guarantee to save you at least three times our fee or your money back."* If you are good enough to offer that kind of guarantee, Economy will never be a problem in your referral equation.

If you are disinclined to make an offer like this, your best bet is to utilize testimonials, statistics or both. For example, *"our average client saves over $200,000 in their first year using our service.*" You have to be careful however because even without a guarantee, most customers will expect to receive something as good or better than average.

Example 15 – Many new or unfamiliar products (those with high Novelty) may encounter difficulties in the perception of their value. As an example, Piano Wizard, a keyboard and software product that can train children as young as three or four to play the piano efficiently in a very few lessons may seem more expensive than a simple keyboard with light-up keys or a software package that teaches kids to read music.

The value is only completely apparent once the child plays their first song. There is not really a good way to put a value on the satisfaction for both the parent and the child in that moment. The value for this product, it's Economy, is only clear after the fact but for referral purposes, that can be even better than the perception of a bargain before the sale is made. In terms of referrals, getting more than you bargained for, *lagniappe* (a little something extra) never hurts.

Example 16 – There was a client in the computer consulting business. His clients used to pay high fees for his expertise five years ago, however, as times have changed he has been forced to justify his fees. When the initial Novelty wears off how do you rebuild it? In this case, it is a highly competitive field that is very saturated with consultants. Probably the best Novelty is again going to be providing a variety of choices in the area of pricing.

Everybody else is offering a straight bid or one option. Offer them a full boat price where he actually has someone camp on their premises permanently which is a very high quote. Give them a lowball price which is way down there but offers very little in the way of services. And then offer one in the middle, which is the one you wanted them to buy to begin with. So, if there is nobody doing menu-driven pricing or nobody doing menu-driven pricing the right way, that could distinguish you for a while.

This is a tough situation because it is a highly commoditized field and very competitive. So he has to work very hard to maintain Novelty but the good news is he doesn't need a lot because he has Utility, Dependability, and Economy. If he is reasonably priced, he needs to keep only about 25% of Novelty to keep you up there for referrals.

Example 17 – There was a client with an herbal extract for hangovers. It has Novelty, Utility, and Dependability, but the Economy is the problem. It's an expensive extract to produce but it is highly effective. You've absolutely, positively got to have Dependability. People are very skeptical of claims for over-the-counter products. There have been a lot of over-the-top and extravagant claims. If there is anything that you can say that affirms the Dependability by independent scientific testing, that helps a little bit. If your Economy is not there, then you have to balance it with a really, really high Dependability. For this product, it will be exceptionally tough because a satisfied user basically has to acknowledge they drank too much to begin with. Outside of fraternity and bachelor parties, this is not a claim most people are eager to confess.

SECTION FOUR

OPERATIONAL DISTINCTIONS

P.M.S. Makes It All Flow Together

Now that you have the fundamental characteristics that people use to determine whether they will look good by referring something or not, you are ready to start learning about the applications principles. Like most of our stuff, it is an acronym that we hope you will find easy to remember.

Although its more famous twin has a somewhat unpleasant reputation there is an interesting similarity between the two synacronyms (two acronyms that have the exact same letters but mean something different - if this is not a real word it needs to be.). Overlooking either P.M.S. can get you in a lot of trouble.

Here is a simple rhyme to help you remember which one is which:

P.M.S. for N.U.D.E.
All right dude
P.M.S. for her
Back off Sir

Hopefully in the future our P.M.S. will be more famous. I am not betting any money on this however.

Perception
M
S

P = Perception

As we've already stated, everything is about perception. But how can we be accountable for what other people perceive? Well, that boils down mostly to what you might call framing or context. Perceptions almost never develop in a vacuum. They are a function of the setting in which they occur, intellectually, socially and physically.

Consider how your perception of an entertainer might shift as a function of the audience you are a part of. If the crowd is large, enthusiastic and supportive, your impression, even if you do not like the artist, tends to be significantly more favorable. On the other hand, even if you are a fan of the entertainer performing, if there are few people and they do not seem interested or impressed, your perception of the entertainer may not go down but it certainly is not likely to improve either.

As to the physical setting, this is pretty obvious but still critical. Everything about the space in which you are first exposed to a product or service potentially has impact on the perception. Details that might seem to have little or no bearing on perceptions, let alone outcomes can in fact make an enormous difference.

One simple but commonplace example is the little offices at car dealerships where they take you to close the deals and arrange the car financing. These can have a remarkably detrimental effect on perceptions of service and value. Because the space is typically at a premium these vestibules are usually quite small and to further compound this cramped image they often have lower ceilings. You might say this type of space could engender a perception of privacy or intimacy. In actual tests however, the primary feeling experienced by most customers is one of being trapped and having little freedom.

> People make decisions best when experiencing a sense of freedom

In any situation where people are being asked to make important decisions, a sense of freedom, of movement and of space, enhances their confidence and the probability of an affirmative choice. Large comfortable swivel chairs on wheels invariably improve success rates when compared to Spartan, low back, 4-leg chairs commonly used for short-term guests in offices. It is an obvious perception once you think about it. Physical freedom of movement is transposed self-consciously into freedom of choice.

I can hear car dealers and other businesses with small spaces for customer interactions kicking, screaming and cursing my name as their sales people righteously point out this section. Let me say to all of you who do not have room or who do not have the budget, if a 10-15% increase in your closing rate would not help you solve those two problems then do not worry about it. There are many other things in this book that will make a difference that don't take up any additional space.

Regarding social settings, continuing with the example of car dealerships, generally speaking, there is no particular reason people should be more likely to purchase cars on a weekend but year-after-year, all across the country, we do. While it is hard to imagine a more solitary or less social experience than buying a car, it has been demonstrated with amazing statistical consistency that people are more prone to buy cars when they sense other people are doing so at the same location. Remarkably, this phenomenon is more clearly correlated with sales than just about any other factor. In point of actual fact, it is generally easier to get a better deal on just about any other day other than a weekend. But even something as notoriously price-sensitive as a car purchase is still surprisingly responsive to the perception generated by a "buying crowd."

The perception that others are willing to go ahead and take the plunge is a simple but soothing notion to most of us. True or not, the perception is clearly that there is indeed safety in numbers.

As one more example, a company had created a service to buy or sell anything using your cell phone (tag lines –" a new way to pay" or "remote control for your money"). This is so unfamiliar that most people are not going to be able to think of an application for it so you are going to have to help the customer. Why would I want to use this service?

People like to feel safe and comfortable

One of the things that people love to talk about is things that make you safer or things that address their particular problems. Let's say I was flying and my luggage did not make it to my destination. I could get a suit, a tie, a shirt and some shoes delivered to the hotel without leaving the lobby.

In social networks one of the most common conversations you hear are warning conversations like the story about a woman who was offered a perfume sample in a parking lot and then was drugged and dragged into a car. Whether that ever happened or not, it goes through social networks like crazy. Cautionary messages, especially about unfamiliar dangers or risks travel through social networks like wild fire. Anything that makes people more comfortable in going somewhere or staying somewhere would be a great example of the value of this service.

If you could just tell people how to solve problems that people worry about all the time like a lost wallet, lost checks, lost luggage, etc. Tell them how to address these problems and they will go ahead and extrapolate it into other applications.

Some of the hardest products and services to sell are those that address an issue that people have become so accustomed to they no longer think of it as a problem. Having to go into a store to buy something, for example, or even to have to go online to order something does not really occur for most people as an inconvenience, let alone a problem. As discussed earlier, most people had no interest in such now ubiquitous things as VCR's, answering machine, and ATM's. That is to say they had no interest until enough other people owned them and used them.

There are hundreds of ways that we have observed how social and physical settings influence perceptions. We cannot cover them all in this book nor would we want to. Understanding the source of perceptions is a large part of what our consultancy thrives on. I think this gives you enough to start thinking about it. Just bear in mind always that perceptions, to one degree or another, are always up for grabs.

Good News & Bad News

The good news is you do not have to manage them perfectly, just better than your competition. The bad news is your competition can probably afford this book too. The good news is they may not be able to afford me as a consultant.

Perception
Message
S

M = The Message

Marshall McLuhan famously observed that: "the medium is the message." In regards to referral marketing, however, where people are the medium it would also be accurate to say "*the medium eats the message*." What we are going to talk about here is how to construct messages in tasty, bite-sized portions that make the referring party look good.

A message that is well suited to referral marketing has to be much more like a tasty snack than a 7-course meal. In regards to the **Looking Good Message (LGM)**, it is helpful to keep reminding yourself of Einstein's axiom that "*things should be made as simple as possible, but no simpler.*"

> They do it to look good

Many businesses, probably most in fact, make the egregious mistake of assuming that someone who is satisfied with their products or services will want to tell others ALL about it. Nothing could be further from the truth. Remember why people refer you; they do it to look good. Long-winded, arduous explanations do not make anyone look good.

As a case in point: it is a little known fact that Alan Greenspahn and Sean Connery are actually twin brothers. Well, no, not really but consider listening to Sean Connery delivering an Alan Greenspahn speech. He would get physically uglier. I promise.

In matters of looking good brevity is indeed, as the old proverb goes, the soul of wit. We want to be clear, concise and to the point when developing a message for your customers to use in distinguishing you in alignment with the N.U.D.E. Model. If it is the least bit complicated, it cannot be conveyed clearly by a large enough number of people. If it is unclear, it does not look good; it is just that simple.

The very simplest way for your customers to speak about you when they refer you is in the context of a result, which needs to be simple but more importantly specific.

Some old advertising slogans are a good example of this: *"Wisk gets out ring-around-the-collar."* This was especially good in those halcyon days of the June Cleaver-ish housewife. Imagine the embarrassment at your lack of domestic engineering proficiency should your husband's collars show that nasty collar stain? It did not take much to get the job done. The ubiquitous Verizon ad *"can-you-hear-me-now"* guy very plainly addresses the issue of cell coverage area. *"But Scott, these are mass media ads;"* you might rightly observe. Yes, but they are effective mass media ads that are so simple they have entered the vernacular and that is exactly the kind of awareness and compactness that we are looking for.

Mass media style messages can work at the person-to-person referral level just as messages suitable for face-to-face delivery can be effective in mass media.

What we will call our **Looking Good Message** or **LGM** for short is not necessarily a verbatim quote or tagline. It is essentially the thing you want people to mention when they endorse you. This is where you will use what you learned in the earlier chapters to identify and construct a powerful **LGM**. We further discuss LGM in Section Four.

By now you must realize how fond I am of using examples to make a point. We had a client with software that impacts the customers' use of the Internet and email. They were technical people trying to explain how it works to sell the product.

Nobody gives a crap about process. I'm going to say it again. NOBODY GIVES A CRAP ABOUT PROCESS. They don't care how it happens. They care what happens.

> Nobody gives a crap about process

So, what are the results? This applies to most businesses. The "before and after" is very important in describing your product or service. What was it like before and then what is it like after your product is installed or utilized? So, you could say that before this product I spent about 90 minutes a day managing my email and after installing your software I can spend about 15 minutes a day on email. Now that proves something. Now it is still a little bit mysterious. We have to eliminate as much of the mystery as possible without referring to process. So we need to find an analogy that will help make it clear. This product is like a sieve for priorities or our product is to email like a microwave is to a cooking, it speeds up the process with a push of the button.

You have to have a very concise message that tells exactly what it is like with your product's results. Your Novelty resides in the result and people being able to think they know how it works. To the degree that they think they know how it works; they are ready to refer it. To the degree that it is so confusing that someone asks them a question about how it works and they can't explain it, do they look good? No. You have to be able to manage the perception in a way that people can convey it to someone else clearly and simply and look good doing it.

The Looking Good Message (LGM)

Generally, the area where you are strongest, i.e.: Novelty, Economy, etc. should be the core of your **Looking Good Message (LGM).**

Your Looking Good Messages are measured in results!

Of course the ideal thing is for your customers to come up with their own **LGM** and to find several of them. You can learn what they have told others simply by asking new customers where they heard about you and what was said. Don't be surprised or upset if it is not what you would have told someone. Just remember that no matter how lame, inaccurate or mundane it may seem to you, you are hearing it from a new customer, so it got the job done. When it comes to **LGM's**, results are all that matter.

A simple exercise that might help you understand the nature of an **LGM** is to look at your own referral behavior for other products or services. For example: many people notice that they mention the same types of characteristics whenever they refer something. They are the types of things that you are personally attuned to. It might be excellent service, innovation, organization, visual appeal, etc. What you may start to see here is that an **LGM** has as much to do with your focus and interest as it does with the product or service itself. All that means is very few businesses are able to enjoy significant referral activity with just one **LGM**.

It really wouldn't be a problem to have as many **LGM's** as you have customers. The truth is when people look good talking about your business they will find lots of different ways to bring it up.

As a personal example: I've been telling people about a favorite restaurant of mine in San Francisco for years. It comes up any time the subject of garlic or spicy food enters a conversation or if I am in a restaurant that offers garlic, I always mention "The Stinking Rose" (their motto is "we season all our garlic with food"). What I tell people about them is that if you are in San Francisco you can find a cab to get you there but it is almost impossible to get a cab to pick you up because when you leave you positively reek of garlic. Now that may not sound like an **LGM** to many of you, but to garlic lovers it is like a red cape to a bull. They can't wait to go there.

Candidly I doubt this is exactly what the owners of "The Stinking Rose" hope their customers are saying about them but among the garlic lovers I have shared this with over the years, the almost universal response has been *"I have got to go there!"* At the risk of sounding like a broken record, what works is all that matters.

As another example: when I was younger I worked in the largest retail liquor store in Oklahoma. It was huge and they had literally every wine, beer and spirit available in the state at that time. The owner always emphasized their excellent prices and they were very competitive but in all the years I worked there, the thing that I heard people say over and over about the store was what a great selection we had. I always found that more than a little amusing in that 90% of our sales were basically from the same 10% of the labels that could be found in any corner liquor store. In fact, most of that "great selection" was just window dressing.

There were things there no one ever bought and that was actually not just okay, it was great. It meant people saw things there not available anywhere else. That just added to the perception we had that *"XYZ store has an incredible selection that can't be found anywhere else."* The truth, of course, was that we had acquired a lot of crap over the years that we were just too lazy to mark down and get rid of but hey, if it works, go with it, right?

As a rule, superlatives (adjectives like "incredible" or "amazing") don't make for great **LGM's** unless they include some reference for comparison, such as:

"*The most incredible selection in the Midwest*"

Or "*the most amazing collection of spatula's in the world.*"

It may not be very chic or trendy but I am more than willing to tell people why I shop at Wal-Mart. It is a great example of Contextual Novelty (discussed in Section Two) but it is also Economy. Wal-Mart has a longstanding policy they seldom advertise and I have found many people are unaware of. They will match any competitor's ad for any item. Dallas is a very competitive retail market, especially for groceries but if I went to every single store to get the best prices on every item it would take forever. Instead I trundle into Wal-Mart with a handful of competitor's ads having already highlighted the best prices in each one. On an average bimonthly shopping trip this saves me at least $30 to $50 every time.

That is not an **LGM** that would work for everyone but because I am notoriously thrifty (aka cheap). I have no hesitation in sharing that **LGM**. Notice that in this case it has worked to Wal-Mart's advantage to keep the policy relatively low profile. If they had advertised it or everyone already knew about it, I would have been deprived of a perfectly good **LGM**.

Referrals and the Internet:

Mostly, the N.U.D.E. model is about face-to-face referrals. Video email, at the point this book was written, has not exactly caught on like wildfire. Video web-conferencing could also hardly be considered ubiquitous. If either of those things ever catches on more widely, web-based referrals could become more of a factor.

The problem with email referrals is that the satisfaction just is not there. There is no direct feedback. If looking good is the reward, eyeball-to-eyeball or at least voice-to-voice is going to be the dominant mode of transmission.

You have got to be face-to-face because if I do it to look good, I want to be looking at you when I tell you about it. I want the gratification when you say: "*Wow, I want to try that!*" I don't get that on email.

There is a very specific strategy for going viral on the Internet. It can be incredibly effective if executed flawlessly. For a number of reasons, however, I am not going to share in this book. It is one of those strategies that once widely known, its impact would be substantially compromised.

Show and Tell

When you are dealing with a physical product, the simplest thing to do is demonstrate it. Show people how it works. This is what we call the **Show-and-Tell LGM.** Whether you have a new cell phone, computer, boat, jewelry, etc., just simply calling attention to it creates an opportunity for a referral. Companies with tangible and especially wearable products are fortunate to benefit from many referrals of this type.

Companies with non-wearable or intangible products should definitely consider promotional products that are wearable, i.e. wristwatch with a car, a nice key chain fob for an insurance company, a very nice pen for a realtor. It is a simple thing but if it creates an opportunity for an **LGM**, it is money well spent.

Perception
Message
Support

S = Support

You are managing the perceptions. You are creating lots of LGM opportunities. What is left to assure optimal referrals?

The "S" in P.M.S. stands for Support. You want to support referring parties as consistently and effectively as possible. A lot of people will think that I mean give them incentives in exchange for their endorsements. Nothing could be further from the truth. I am sure many people would be surprised to learn that I am generally opposed to referral incentives; given that many, if not most customer referral programs are based on what amounts to institutionalized bribery.

It is really only remarkable that few businesses have noticed how poorly these programs usually perform. There are really only two common outcomes for most customer referral programs. The first is that you will have only a very few mercenary souls willing to prostitute their credibility in exchange for some small kickback or compensation. Obviously enough these are the people whose credibility generally has too little leverage to influence those who know them.

The second and even less desirable outcome occurs when a natural referral, one that would have been given anyway is compensated after the fact. All too often this is done in such a way that it makes the referring party feel somehow guilty or complicitous. It puts them in an awkward position where they may even feel a little dirty because they have made money off a friend. Either without their knowledge which is like lying to a friend or if they choose to disclose the incentive, it renders their credibility suspect. So, with very few exceptions, I am opposed to any kind of substantive compensation.

Please do not hear that as suggesting that you should not express your gratitude. I am a huge fan of acknowledgement. I even train people in effective acknowledgement and it is the subject of our next book. But money or other things of value do not, of themselves, denote either gratitude or acknowledgement.

It is a looking good thing!

For the umpteenth time let me remind you why people refer things. They do it to look good and for most of us that is more than compensation enough.

If we look, it is apparent that most of our lives are consumed with this compulsion to polish and shape our image for others. Our spouses, our careers, our homes, our cars, and the clothes we buy, nearly everything you can say, down to the way we speak is all a part of that finely crafted strategy for our personal image enhancement. Given all that and the fact that referring you is going to make them look good, why pollute the issue with compensation of any kind. Undoubtedly at this point those of you with incentivized customer referral programs are protesting vehemently that your program works. Please note, I never said that compensated referrals don't work at all; I'm just saying that they don't work as well as uncompensated referrals designed inside the N.U.D.E. Model.

If you would rather continue paying for something that we can show you how to get more of for free, please don't let me be the one to dissuade you. In passing, however, you may want to note that the big three for referrals: books, movies and restaurants seldom, if ever, offer any kind of cash compensation for referrals.

It is counterintuitive (I like that word and use it a lot. It is geek for "surprised the beans out of me") but there are just some things people do better for free than for money or rewards. Referrals are one of them.

What is support?

Now we have said what support is NOT. What then is it?

Basically, support, in the context of referrals, is making sure your customers get what they wanted when they sent you the business in the first place. By now, hopefully we all know what that is. They want to look good and your job is to make sure they do with every new customer. This is going to be easier for some businesses than others and I am going to start with some really basic stuff. A few of these things, I am sure a lot of you know instinctively already. I am amazed though at how often even those who know better leave out these small but important steps.

So even you "old hands" at customer service may want to take some time with this section and make sure nothing has slipped through the cracks.

The first and foremost thing to do with every new customer is, whenever possible recognizing and acknowledge them as such. This is easier obviously for small businesses and well nigh impossible for someone the size of Wal-Mart (although their greeters and standard saying "thank you for shopping at Wal-Mart" are nice touches).

Plainly enough if you have a product that is sold off the shelf you don't have to worry about this part but even there it is often advisable to offer some form of customer support such as an 800 phone number for a help desk or at least a website with FAQ's.

If you are delivering face-to-face service, especially professional or personal services you want to take a moment to get acquainted with each new customer and sincerely show your appreciation for their patronage. If you are the proprietor or manager it is often effective to give them your card and let them know you are available if there is ever anything you can help them with. Again, I realize this is pretty basic stuff but notice how many businesses fail to exercise this simple and effective practice.

If you are an absentee owner or in your place of business only infrequently, another way to provide support that assures people who refer, they will look good, is to let people know when you are always there, such as:

> "*I'm always in my office every Monday and Wednesday morning*"
> Or "*I'm usually in my office on the 1st and 15th of the month.*"

This serves a couple of purposes. First, it is the kind of insider information that naturally makes people look good. They know when they can see the owner. Secondly, it helps to serve that all-important perception of Dependability.

If you are fortunate enough to be personally acquainted with most of your clients or customers you will usually recognize a new one. Here's a great opportunity to make your existing client look good. As soon as you know an existing client referred someone say something nice that you really mean about the referring party. It could be how long they have been doing business with you, it could be something complimentary about their children or even some personal minor detail like "*boy, he really likes to golf doesn't he?*" This does much more than just makes the referring party look good - it makes you look good. It makes it clear that you have an interest in your customers that goes beyond what they buy from you.

A lot of business owners automatically expect their friends to be their customers but quite a few of those same people are not concerned enough with having their customers as friends. Giving people just a little personal care and attention is the simplest and easiest way to make the referring party look good.

You can find just about any business in the yellow pages or on the Internet but you are much more likely to find relationship as a result of a referral. For those of you who supply products, especially where there is no human interface at all, such as via the Internet or wholesale, you can include an element of personal relationship by just remembering to use people's names in email interactions and doing an occasional phone follow-up.

Another basic element of making the referred party look good is to be easy to do business with. For one simple example, look at the type of information you ask of your customers. How much do you really need to know? What information that you collect do you really use? More importantly will they understand why you are asking them for any particular information and respect your need to have it?

Avoid the "P" word

As another quick example, never use the "P" word in any customer interaction unless you are sincerely interested in losing their business. Many companies throw the "P" word around off-handedly as if it were as acceptable as *"please"* or *"thank you."* The word ***"Policy"*** in North American English generally means:

> *"You are not going to get what you want and there is nothing I am willing or able to do about it."* You may as well say: *"grab your ankles."*

This is such an ingrained reaction starting from early childhood, for most of us, that few people can even recall anything said after the phrase

> *"Our policy is..."*

You could say,

> *"Our policy is to give you a million dollars, your own personalized parking space and three wishes which we must grant."*

And they would be thinking about calling their attorney because they already think they know what is coming, and it is never good.

Now did I say you shouldn't have policies? No, absolutely not. You obviously have to have systems and rules for dealing with customers and employees but if you want them to hear what they are, begin by saying:

> "*The way we usually handle that ...*"
>
> Or "*may I please go over our options in this circumstance ...*"
>
> Or "*we have found this way works best ...*"

We have attempted to be as comprehensive as possible but freely acknowledge there will be many circumstances and types of businesses that we have not fully addressed here. We welcome your questions via email but apologize that we may not be able to answer each one in detail. In particular, we are generally unwilling to address hypothetical questions. If you have had a particular experience or problem applying the N.U.D.E. Model, a detailed description is helpful but we cannot *answer "what if"* and *"how to"* questions and still attend to our business.

The best way to get results from this book is to just get started. If you like the ideas and agree with the principles but are having a hard time thinking about how to put them into practice, we highly recommend Guy Kawasaki's book ***"The Art of the Start"*** or for more about referral marketing read ***"The Secrets of Word-of-Mouth Marketing***" by George Silverman.

To learn more about our consulting and speaking services, please go to www.NecessaryMeasures.com

SECTION FIVE

WORKSHEETS

The N U D E Worksheet

Apply what you have learned to your product or service and what work there is for you to do to obtain viral marketing.

Novelty:
Unfamiliar, not widely known.
Your Score
_________%
Max. 100%

Describe your **Novelty** Driver & the customers' perceptions:

____

____

Utility:
Satisfies a need for the listener.
Your Score
_________%
Max. 100%

Describe your **Utility** Driver & the customers' perceptions

____

____

Dependability:
Confidence of performance.
Your Score
_________%
Max. 100%

Describe your **Dependability** Driver & the customers' perceptions:

____

____

Economy:
Reduces time, cost, etc.
Your Score
_________%
Max. 100%

Describe your **Economy** Driver & the customers' perceptions:

____

____

Your Total NUDE Score _________%
Max. 400%

What ideas could you implement to enhance your score?

____

____

____

The P M S Worksheet

P

What are the customers' **perceptions** of your product or service?

____
____
____

What can you provide to add more **perceptions** of safety & freedom?

____
____
____

M

What **message** are customers giving when referring your product?

____
____
____

What is the Looking Good **Message** used by your customers?

____
____
____

S

How do you **support** your customers' that refer your product or service?

____
____
____

What **support** given so customers look good when referring your product?

____
____
____

What actions will you implement to move your product or service into viral referral marketing?

Key Steps	**Completion Date**

SECTION SIX

WHERE DO WE GO FROM HERE?

Scott and Donna offer a wide range of consulting services including, but not limited to, referral marketing strategies for almost any type of business. Their consulting promise is to increase your referral customer base by at least 300% or continue working with you until that result is achieved. They work with businesses ranging from home-based start-ups to global corporations and everything in between.

Scott is also widely known for his work in employee and customer retention. His unblemished ten-year record is to have reduced voluntary employee turnover by no less than 50% without recourse to compensation or other recurring costs. His concept of "tenure equity" has been referenced as the most important new business metric in years.

Their next book, already in progress, will focus on the importance of acknowledgment in relationships. It will demonstrate how the Five Languages of Acknowledgment (Trust, Respect, Appreciation, Interest and Listening) can bring satisfaction, fulfillment and new levels of achievement to corporations, families, organizations and communities.

Both Scott and Donna are available as keynote speakers and seminar presenters. For more information contact sdegraffenreid@aol.com.

INDEX

"

"how to" questions.... 113

A

Acknowledgment...... 121
advertising.. 7, 11, 13, 14, 15, 16, 17, 19, 22, 23, 24, 88, 102
alternative medicine.... 25
ATM............. 60, 85, 100

B

Behavior Analysis......... 7
Behavioral Statistician 24
Behavioral Statistics. 4, 6, 7
Bernoulli Principle...... 27
Bottle Rocket............. 40
breakthrough product. 64, 65, 66

C

car dealers.................. 98
carpet cleaning 57, 58, 78
Challenging Referrals. 69
cheaper........... 41, 48, 61
Class A referrals.... 53, 58
Clueless Agents.......... 79
competition... 31, 76, 100
computer consulting.... 94
consultants. 69, 70, 88, 94
Contextual Novelty30, 31
countertops...... 76, 77, 78

D

De Ja Vu...................... 66
decision matrix............ 61
Dependability. 36, 37, 38, 39, 40, 42, 45, 46, 47, 49, 50, 54, 55, 56, 58, 60, 61, 62, 64, 69, 70, 74, 75, 76, 81, 87, 89, 90, 91, 93, 95, 111
diads............... 35, 59, 61
doctor.. 39, 54, 70, 72, 75
drivers.. 8, 28, 50, 51, 62, 68, 69, 75, 86, 90
dry cleaning.......... 43, 92

E

Economic Buyer.... 79, 80
Economy.. 41, 42, 43, 48, 49, 50, 55, 58, 60, 61, 62, 64, 69, 70, 71, 75, 76, 81, 92, 93, 94, 95, 103, 106
Economy of Relationship 43

Edward DeBono............ 9
Einstein 9, 101
endorsement... 17, 20, 23, 47, 64
End-User 79, 80
exponential.................. 51
extraordinary guarantee 46, 54, 76, 87, 88
Extraordinary Guarantees.. 9, 45, 87

F

Feng Shui 81
Fresh Novelty.. 30, 31, 44
FUD............................. 93
furniture........... 40, 58, 81

G

gas station.................... 42
Gimme's...................... 78
Good News/Bad News64, 65
Good, better, best 88
good-fast-cheap........... 61
graphic designers 88

H

helicopters 12
Human behavior............ 5
Human Resource......... 93
Hummer 41

I

IBI Global x
incentives 10

incidence of acceptance 20, 21, 23
incidence of consideration19, 20, 21
insider information.... 111
Invisible........................ 82

L

LGM... 81, 101, 102, 103, 104, 105, 106, 107, 108
looking good .. 26, 64, 67, 101, 107
Looking Good Message ... 80, 81, 101, 102, 103
Looking Good Referrals 70
loyalty 11, 43

M

Managed Care 70
market research 59, 60
marketing campaign.... 17
mattresses.................... 86
MLM........................... 52
money-back guarantee 38, 45, 46, 61
movies....... 7, 21, 83, 109

N

N.U.D.E. Model .. i, 2, 28, 51, 63, 69, 101, 109, 113
N.U.D.E. score51, 56, 58, 76
natural referral........... 108

Novelty29, 30, 31, 33, 34, 35, 36, 40, 44, 49, 50, 53, 54, 55, 56, 58, 59, 60, 62, 63, 64, 66, 69, 70, 71, 74, 75, 76, 77, 78, 80, 81, 82, 84, 85, 87, 91, 93, 94, 95, 103, 106
nutritional supplement 87

O

Outcome-driven Referrals ... 71
Outlet malls ... 48

P

P.M.S ... 96, 108
Parkinson's ... xi
People are the New Media ... 16
perception. 27, 33, 34, 38, 39, 40, 45, 46, 48, 52, 57, 58, 60, 61, 62, 64, 74, 77, 91, 93, 94, 97, 98, 99, 103, 105, 111
perceptions ix, 27, 39, 45, 48, 52, 56, 92, 97, 100, 108
pharmaceutical company ... 6, 24, 25
poisoned well ... 38
Policy ... 112
Pres Que Vu ... 66
private investigation service ... 84
promotional products . 72, 107
puppy dog close ... 84

R

real estate ... 90
referral behavior. 7, 8, 24, 28, 44, 49, 50, 52, 53, 55, 61, 69, 74, 79, 104
referral business ... 56
refund ... 76
Requested Referrals 70
restaurants .. 7, 20, 33, 34, 35, 36, 39, 55, 74, 77, 109
retail 37, 48, 105, 106

S

Show-and-Tell ... 107
Social Network Analysis ... 4, 5, 7, 8, 13, 51
Social Network Analyst4, 69
Social Network Marketing ... 47
social settings ... 98
software product ... 94
Spam ... 64
survey research ... 23

T

take it or leave it.... 88, 89
Tangible Reminders 72
TANSTAAFL Paradox ... 63, 64, 65, 66

The Life Vessel............ xi
time-share.................... 88
tipping point... 50, 51, 52, 74
Tipping Point 50
tipping points 51, 87
tool organizer........ 78, 80
Toxic..................... 64, 66
transparent................... 42
TV show...................... 60

U

undifferentiated........... 42
Utility. 32, 33, 34, 35, 38, 44, 49, 50, 52, 54, 55, 56, 57, 58, 59, 60, 62, 64, 69, 70, 71, 75, 76, 81, 84, 85, 86, 87, 91, 93, 95

V

Vacation destinations.. 70
VCR 60, 100
viral ...vii, viii, 17, 21, 25, 30, 44, 46, 49, 50, 51, 52, 107
viral referral strategy... 44

W

wait and see................. 90
web-based referrals ... 106
what if................ 12, 113
Wright brothers....... 5, 12